Firewalk

Transcending the Fear
Awakening to Love

---

by Patricia Bateson

al Peace i love. joy to you on your journey. Enjoy the ride

First published in the United States of America by Patricia Bateson 2015

Some names of individuals in this book have been changed to protect their identity. The exceptions are those people that granted permission to freely use their names.

All quotations of other works reproduced are done so either with the permission of the original author, or are quoted and attributed under fair use.

Bateson, Patricia
ISBN: 0692276149
ISBN-13: 978-0692276143 (EAN)

First printing: 2015
Printed in the United States of America
Set in PT Serif

First Edition: 2015

"Healers are spiritual warriors who have found the courage to defeat the darkness of their souls. Awakening and rising from the depths of their fears, like a Phoenix rising from the ashes. Reborn with a wisdom and strength that creates a light that shines bright enough to help, encourage, and inspire others out of their own darkness."

Melanie Koulouris

WITH GRATITUDE

So many loving souls have contributed to the birthing of my book, including family members, close friends, acquaintances, teachers, and healers. To each of you I offer my humble appreciation. Without a shred of doubt, you are my angels!

I wish to express special gratitude to:

Cheryl Davey, Judith Fogarty, Michael Redsky, Marilyn Hutnick, Joanne Mirra, for your beautifully written contributions.

Sheri Horn Hasan: my inspiring editor.

Chelsea Stearns: my creative designer.

Marilyn, Joanne and Dan: My beloved sisters and brother. You are my heart and soul for all eternity. A special bond we share, that can never be broken.

Colleen, Erin and Patrick James: My three cherubs! You are and always will be the "lights of my life!" Each of you is magnificent in your own unique way. I love you all!

Todd: You have been my rock, my soft place to fall, my everything. For sticking with, and never giving up on me - you are the most amazing husband and you have my heart always.

Mom and Dad: Time and space can never separate us. I feel your presence, your unconditional love and support every day. Thank you for these gifts, as they are indeed rare treasures!

And finally to my Higher Power: For giving me my wings to fly. With you ~~~~~~ **ALL THINGS ARE POSSIBLE!**

A MESSAGE FROM PAT'S ANGELS

We, Patricia's angels, are delighted to come forward to share our perspective of Pat's first of many creations called "**FIREWALK**... Transcending the Fear... Awakening to Love." Pat has shown such strength and resilience through the process of creating this book. She is a shining example of when to allow spirit to come through to help with such difficult and complicated emotions of a family struggling with dependency. Pat was unique to notice that all of these experiences were at the core... and all about **love**, and to allow Pat's soul to grow in a beautiful and powerful awakening process.

We are overjoyed that Pat is prepared and committed to show how the love of self equals the love of a higher power, when working through challenges. Once the love of self is mastered, then love of others comes next. You, as humans, are but a mere physical body with a powerful enough spirit to move mountains outside the scope of any physical possibilities.

Our dearest loved ones, open your hearts to the realm of infinite possibilities for yourself and lean on us... your Creator, angels, and guides. We can comfort, strengthen and shift perspectives, as to overcome any obstacle of the body, mind, and spirit. Nothing is beyond our (spiritual) capabilities; but belief in yourself and your God given abilities is what needs concentration.

This book is so poignantly and delicately written, as it will tug at your heartstrings to create peace within. The wonderful thing (about looking within and having faith in a higher power) is that **acknowledgment, forgiveness, and love equals peace**... It is through Pat's efforts and dedication to help others that she in turn helped heal herself, demonstrating the beauty of what it is like to heal old wounds. The joy that comes from "*letting go of old baggage*" is an extraordinary gift to give yourself.

Your soul has asked to incarnate on this earth to seek clarity and wisdom. Perhaps it is time for the **REAL** you to emerge and enjoy the life you came here to live!

Love and Blessings,
From your Angels

This beautiful message was received and channeled from Patricia's angels and guides, as a loving gesture done by Cheryl Davey, a friend and soul sister on this spiritual journey. Feel free to visit her website **WhisperedByAngels.com***.*

CONTENTS

Foreword

Albert Einstein once said: "There are only two ways to live your life. One is as though nothing is a miracle. The other is as if everything is."

At the beginning stages of my cancer I felt like a *victim*. Thought I was the only one on the planet who felt this way. *Poor Pat: The underdog, the pansy, the chump--everything bad always happens to her!*

I have since spoken with hundreds of cancer survivors and found that many express the same thought. They ask questions like: "What could I have done differently to prevent this?" Or "what did I do to cause this disease?" The attempt to come to grips with our new friend *cancer* turns our world upside down and inside out in a matter of seconds.

What's of even greater import, though, involves figuring out how to work through the emotions associated with *why me?* and to move on. After all, how likely was it I'd ever figure out why I got this disease? Wasn't it a waste of precious time and energy better spent toward my recovery and healing process?

I learned the hard way that living life as if everything is a miracle brings personal growth, while existing with the notion that nothing about life is miraculous left me feeling stagnant and stuck. Ultimately, I chose to understand the difference between these radically opposed responses.

Eventually, I recognized that to heal is to return to wholeness, and I vowed to make that my intention and my mission.

Firewalk

Introduction
The Phone Call

Have you ever wanted something so badly you could taste it, feel it--perhaps even *will* it to happen?

Sweet Lord, why isn't he calling me back? It's been two long, excruciating days just waiting with bated breath for this one phone call! Is one silly phone call too much to ask? I don't think so because I need to know! But I don't want to know. Yet, I must know...

My palms sweat and my stomach flip-flops as it spits out enough acid to create a crater-sized ulcer. That queasy, unsettled feeling in the pit of my gut is reminiscent of when I was pregnant. But I'm not pregnant--that's a definite!

I make a half-hearted attempt to eat a piece of wheat toast with Smucker's grape jelly on it, but my body recoils. The smell alone repulses me, and my throat constricts as if to say, "*no*, not now!" The toast wins! I toss the remnants in the barrel before I completely lose it.

Seven minutes go by since I last looked at the digits on the telephone. I'm getting to know every nook and cranny of "Ma Bell" real well. *Perhaps I should call the office again...maybe my doctor is not receiving my messages! Doesn't he know I'm on pins and needles? Doesn't he care that I can barely function or focus on my daily tasks?*

I pick up the phone and contemplate another urgent call, but decide to wait. It's been only an hour since I spoke to the answering service last. *Be patient,* I tell myself. I try, but it's damn hard! *I just need to know my test results!*

I decide to put on one of my favorite game shows, *Wheel of Fortune,* but today perky Pat and glamorous Vanna are driving me up a wall. Who cares about a brand new Jeep Cherokee or a round trip for two to Ireland? Not *me!*

I mimic a contestant who's screaming at the top of her lungs because there are three S's in the puzzle. *I don't care if there are twenty S's or if the entire puzzle is spelled with the letter S! What a silly show--it should be called Wheel of Misfortune!* I surf channels mindlessly, but nothing appeals to me. I shut it off with a click, and find odd pleasure in staring at a blank screen.

"I just need peace and quiet," I mumble. "That will help." Standing up to stretch, I let out a huge sigh. *I can't believe how tired I feel. Well, you did just have a lumpectomy two days ago,* I remind myself. I sneak a quick peek under my tank top to check my left breast. She is swollen and discolored.

"I'm sorry you had to go through this," I tell my breast, "but we had to remove that pea-sized lump. It was growing bigger by the day and it looked very suspicious on ultrasound." I touch my bosom ever so gingerly as if to heal the tender area with love, and then gently lay my top back down.

What now? I contemplate. My head feels fuzzy and my temples pulsate with a throbbing ache similar to a migraine. *Is this headache related to the nausea or the pain that I'm feeling? Do I need to drink more fluids or eat something? I've tried, but I just can't! Perhaps I need to lie down and rest. What is my body trying to tell me? I haven't a clue--I'm not a god damn psychic!*

I trudge aimlessly with heavy feet from room to room. I don't know what to do. I don't know where to go. I find myself staring at the phone again. A whopping twenty minutes have passed since my last time check.

Ring, you darn phone! Just ring and let it be my surgeon! Tell me something, anything, to relieve this anxiety--I can't take it any longer! I am going to crack like Humpty Dumpty--you know, that dumb nursery rhyme about a character portrayed as an egg? He sits on a wall, falls off, cracks into a zillion pieces and no one can put him back together...that's gonna be me pretty soon if that phone doesn't ring! I'm gonna crack into a trillion pieces and there will be no putting me back together, either--I just know it!"

Phone in hand, I place the receiver against my ear and imagine different scenarios—one of which I am probably going to hear very soon:

"Hello Patricia, this is Dr. P. I have some wonderful news! Your tumor is benign. There's nothing further you need to do. Have a lovely life."

CLICK

"Hello Patricia, this is Dr. P. I have pretty good news for you. Your tumor did contain some abnormal cells, but there's nothing you need to do right now. We'll keep an eye on it and hope for the best."

CLICK

"Hello Patricia, this is Dr. P. Unfortunately I have bad news for you. You have breast cancer."

CLICK

The last scenario sends a shiver up my spine and an intense feeling of heat surges through my veins. I feel like I'm on fire! I rush to the kitchen sink to put it out with a cold glass of water but my throat refuses it.

"I'm going to be sick!" I scream. I begin to wretch violently and clear phlegm shoots out my mouth and nostrils. It burns the insides of my nose so much that tears start to stream down my face. From the neck up I feel an intense pressure--as though it's wedged in a vise that's growing tighter and tighter. My head feels like it's going to explode. I've never experienced such grotesque pain in my life!

My body twists and contorts and, for what seems like an eternity I writhe in physical and mental pain, but in reality it lasts only a few minutes. I grab a paper towel to wipe the saliva, sweat, and tears that pour out of me, then fall to the linoleum floor in sheer exhaustion. Ironically, I find comfort there as the cold, hard floor feels really good against my drenched, battered body.

This wait is killing me--I'm not good at waiting! Please just call me!

The phone rings and I jump a mile into the air. The adrenaline is flowing fast and furious. It's my daughters calling. Nineteen and twenty-one, respectively, they are very dedicated, compassionate young women.

"Mom, we're coming over!" they jibber jabber to me.

"Okay," I say, even though there's a part of me that just wants to be alone. It's hard enough handling *me* right now, never mind anyone else, but I tell them to come on along.

Hurry up and get dressed, Pat! Throw some water on your face, brush your teeth, and don't forget to put on your cheery face. I don't know if I can pull this off, God. I'm shaking in my boots right now!

The girls arrive and we share small talk for a bit. I sense their anxiety, as I'm sure they sense mine. We talk about their return to college in a few weeks and how much they're both looking forward to new experiences.

It does take my mind off the current situation temporarily, and I actually feel lighter. *College, friends, guys, hanging out--not too shabby, sign me up!* I think. *Wish I was heading off to college, then I wouldn't be in this predicament and life would be just grand...*

Plunked in front of the boob tube again, and not wanting to be a party pooper, the girls and I watch a rerun of *Saved by the Bell.* Must be the hundredth time we've seen this one. Screech and Zack are up to their usual pranks, and Mr. Belding, the principal, is having a nutsy.

"How friggin' corny!" I catch myself saying out loud rather sarcastically. The girls are in hysterics but I merely witness a bunch of figures jumping around on a screen mumbling meaningless words. Nothing makes sense to me right now. Nothing is remotely funny. My mind feels vacant, like nobody is home.

Then, without warning, it happens.

I hear the faint ringing of the telephone. It seems so distant, so far away. I glance over at my daughters. How beautiful and extraordinary they both are--have I told them how much I love them recently? I can't remember. My thoughts suddenly become pure mush and my body feels like it's moving in slow motion.

Pat, get up, the phone is for you! Did you forget? This is the call you've been waiting for! How do you know? I hear from somewhere inside me. *I just do! Hurry up--answer it before he hangs up!*

I don't want to answer it. I'm too frightened. *If I don't pick up, I won't have to find out the results. That will be better. I'd rather not know. Just answer it, you big baby!*

I enter my bedroom, close the door, and gaze down at the telephone. It's the call I've been waiting for. *Oh shit!*

My mind races and my mouth feels really parched like the Sahara Desert in mid-July. My throat tightens and I can barely swallow. Suddenly, no air seems to be passing through my vocal chords. *I don't know if I can speak! What if nothing comes out? He won't know I'm on the other end of the receiver, desperately waiting for his reply--he won't be able to hear me and he'll just hang up! Oh, God... what then?* I suck in all the air I possibly can and proceed to hit the talk button.

"Hello?" I whisper.

"Hello Patricia, this is Dr. P. I apologize for taking so long to get back to you but I wanted to have all your test results in front of me before I made this very important call. Are you sitting down?"

"No," I tell him weakly.

"You may want to," he replies softly.

"Want to sit down?" I sputter under my breath. *Why the heck would I want to sit down?* And then it hits me. Like a brick being thrown against my head at fifty miles an hour, it hits me! The room begins to spin and my body suddenly feels like it weighs two tons--maybe even three. Panic sets in. *Oh God, I can't catch my breath! No air is coming in--I can't breathe!*

"I'm very sorry to tell you this Patricia, but your tumor was malignant. You have *breast cancer*."

He doesn't need to say another word. I've already checked out!

CLICK

Little did I know that this moment would offer me an opportunity to reexamine my life, and help me reclaim my power.

Chapter One
My Grand Entrance

Kids don't know anything. They haven't experienced nothin' yet. Have you heard this before? Join the group.

I can't say I actually recollect sliding down the birth canal and into the doctor's arms covered in blood and mucus, all wet and soggy, looking like a shriveled up old woman who's sat in the bathtub way too long. No, I can't say any of that comes back to me. Sounds too gross, anyway...I probably blocked that part out.

But I do remember one very important detail about my grand entrance into the world. Call it a memory, a hunch, a knowing--it just *was.* It wasn't really anything tangible, something you could put your index finger on and say "that's it!" No, it was nothing like that at all. Something or someone spoke to me from the inside.

Inside of what, you ask? Can't tell you that, either. See, I'm only a newborn baby, what do I know? That day, a little voice bubbled up from within and told me a deep, dark secret. It was a big one alright--it was *ginormous!* That's short for gigantic and enormous combined, just so you know. What that voice told me could have knocked a strapping lumberjack to his knees in an instant; taken him right out, in one fell swoop. That's how powerful it was.

"*You are not wanted!*" the voice said.

What did you just say?

"*You are not wanted!*" the bulletin flashed.

How could that be? I ponder. *Kind of late to tell me now, don't you think?*

Wham, bam, slam, dunk! Let's take the girl out before she barely has a chance to take her first breath! It didn't take me long to understand the meaning of those dreaded words, once the delivery room nurse suctioned the mucus out of my nose and wiped my eyes so I could view my new surroundings. You see, I might have been brand spanking new, but I *was* pretty bright and I could tell plenty from my bassinet. Looks speak for themselves, and I watched Mom and Dad very carefully those first few minutes after birth.

Dad's forehead was tense and tight--the lines of stress ran from one side of his temple to the other. He wasn't smiling, not even a little, as he paced back and forth across the room. Mom's face was ghostly white and her eyelids drooped, as if she wanted to sleep for a year. Heck, she must've been all tuckered out after my wild entrance into the new world!

There I lay in the incubator, wrapped in my warm, pink blanket, waiting for some gentle arms to scoop me up and cozy me into them. *Mom, Dad...would you hold me, kiss me, tickle me-- acknowledge that I'm here? Can anybody see me?* I let out a faint whimper, and guess what?

Nothing...happens.. No one stirs. No one jumps to attention. Something's drastically wrong, that I know. Actions speak volumes and in that instant, even as a brand spanking new baby, I had a knowing. Hard to fathom, I know, but it just was. Something in my heart told me that my dad had hoped for a boy, and I was *not* what he'd anticipated. Matter of fact, I was his third daughter. No wonder he was so discombobulated! Wasn't remotely what he expected or wanted.

But alas, here I am. A precious, adorable, bundle of joy, so full of life and love--ready to take on the world! *Heck, what do I do now? Can I go back the way I came into the world, up the birth canal? Impossible! I can't go back, I'm non-returnable! Guess I'm here to stay, so let's see what happens and hope for the best. Hope for the best...doesn't sound too promising, but it will have to do as it appears I have no other choice.*

That's the beginning of my story--how it all began on that cold wintery day in January 1958.

Chapter Two
Chaos

"Mommy, Mommy, don't leave!" I scream as I watch my mother scurry out the front door of our humble abode. "Please don't leave us, don't leave me!" I plead. *I'm only six years old; I don't know how to take care of me! I don't know how to take care of the family! I'm only a little kid! Who will feed me? Who will take care of me when I'm sick?*

She doesn't respond. She can't hear me. My mother looks like a wild animal cornered in its cage, a predator ready to devour its prey if provoked. Her bug-eyes seem like they might pop out of their sockets. Her lips purse tightly and her jaw clenches shut, as steam spews out of her ears and the top of her head. She is filled with *rage*.

Watch out, I think, *she's gonna blow a gasket! Here we go again!* An all too familiar scene, yet it's never before escalated to this point...never gone quite this far.

"Holy crap, oh God," I whisper to myself. *What's happening? This can't be real! Somebody—anybody--help us! Dad, do something! Stop her!*

My head spins in a million different directions, and I feel

woozy. My stomach jolts up and down and side to side, like when I'm on the tilt-a-whirl at Canobie Lake Park. My body feels jumpy and tingly, cold and numb, all at the same time, though I can palpate each sensation individually. Tears stream down my face faster than I can count, plopping everywhere--all over my yellow cotton shirt, into my brown locks of hair, and onto the hardwood floor. They taste bitter and salty and sting my lips a little. It hurts, but I don't care--I'm used to pain!

I can't think about me right now, anyway. I have to fix this situation! But how can I? I'm only six, remember? I look at the faces of Marilyn and Joanne, my two older sisters, and younger brother Dan, and see in them a mirror of my emotions--sheer terror and impending doom. They are frozen in fear. It is chaos, utter madness, all wrapped up in one neat package.

Dad makes a half-ass attempt to take charge.

"Go sit down on the couch and don't move a muscle!" he yells. We do what he says instantly--we know better, if you know what I mean. We huddle together on the couch, engulfed in each other's embrace. We are *all* that we've got right now. Like refugees on a shipwrecked boat, we cling to each other for dear life, hoping we don't go down with the sinking ship!

Dad begins to yell random stuff at Mom. I despise that--they never talk calmly to each other.

"Rita, don't leave," he pleads. "I'll change, I promise! You'll see! I mean it this time! We'll make this work. Please stay. We *need* you--*I* need you!"

"Go to hell John!" she screams back at him. "I'm *so* sick of your lies! Sick of your promises! Sick of you, and I'm leaving you!"

Leaving? How can she leave us? The thought is staggering. I can't comprehend why my mother would want to leave us, leave *me!* Did I misbehave one too many times? I certainly didn't think so. *I'm almost always on my best behavior,* I think as I conduct a mental review. *I try to be a "good girl" and help with chores around the house. I get good grades. I never get into trouble at school. So, what could I have done that's so bad that Mommy would be forced to leave? There must be something! What, though?*

There is dead silence in the hallway. You can hear a pin drop. For a brief moment—wishful thinking, I know--I pray she has a change of heart.

Please, please, please, Mommy, stay with us! I repeat silently over and over to myself. *I beg of you. I will be good. I promise. We all need you! I love you! Don't go! I'm afraid of Daddy. He doesn't take care of me like you do. He yells at me. He hits me. He doesn't know what to do when I get sick. He doesn't play hide and seek with me. I can't survive without you Mommy! I'd rather die!*

I hear the door handle begin to turn and my sense of

awareness heightens. I spring off the seat of the couch and bolt to the front door. Mom's clutching her suitcase tightly with both hands as she scampers down the five brick steps that lead to our car.

Oh, dear God, she really is going! No-ooo-ooo! Every ounce of blood drains from my face and head and I feel weak all over. My heart pounds to its own beat and it's the scariest feeling I've ever had. I bang on the pane of glass with my fist. I don't care if I break the damn thing. I don't care if I cut myself and bleed all over the putrid green rug in the hallway! I just want my mommy!

Dad attempts to take the suitcase away. He tries to grab her arm to bring her back into the house. She does not want any part of it—or him. He has a dazed look on his face, but you can clearly see he's trying to remain calm. She's leaving *him* too—how can he possibly raise four young children alone? He doesn't have a clue! He needs her desperately and clearly this is a desperate moment. Standing on tiptoes, I strain to get one last glimpse of my mother before she gets into the car. Her face is all distorted, as if she's in a state of confusion. *How can she be?* I wonder. *Clearly she knows what she's doing—she's about to abandon me and my siblings! How can she do this? Please, someone tell me how?*

I feel so alone, so afraid, so *helpless!* Indeed, this is one of the bleakest days of my life. A wall of darkness, designed to keep out all the ugly feelings, settles around my heart. Nothing in my world feels right, and I haven't a friggin' clue what any of this means. The one thing I do know is that this wall provides a temporary shelter to prevent me from collapsing into a sea of utter despair.

"Get your hands off me!" Mom yells at Dad. He retracts them quickly and steps away from her. Mom has the upper hand right now, and he doesn't want to botch things up any more than he has already.

"Rita, I beg of you!" he pleads. "Stay and we'll work this out, I promise!" He is crying hysterically at this point and it's total insanity. Rarely have I seen my dad cry and it fills me with great sadness. Somehow, on some level I have yet to discover, I understand his wounds. Yet there's a part of me that despises him for all the drama he's caused, for all the suffering he's created.

I want to scream, but nothing comes out. My throat is hoarse from sobbing, my head throbs, and my body feels limp. I can't take much more. An ounce of anger seeps into my abdomen and wraps itself around my insides. Where did this come from? It's suffocating it's so tight. It reminds me of a stomach bug I caught last fall when my belly went into spasm and I wretched, then eventually threw up. I hated that feeling then, and I hate it even more now. It feels so wrong. I need to get rid of it immediately!

Without a second thought, I instinctively push that awkward

feeling, that *anger,* deep down inside. Little did I know this was only the beginning of a tainted and sick relationship between my inner child and my higher self.

Somehow, some way, Dad convinces Mom to stay that perilous Sunday afternoon. Is it the right decision for her? Who knows, but she comes back to the "hell hole" anyway, marches in the door, up the stairs to her bedroom, and unpacks her bags. I couldn't have been happier!

Life goes on as usual in the "White House." Oh, did I forget to mention that "White" is my last name and that we live in a white house, too? Everyone, including Dad, is on their best behavior, and not another word is ever spoken about that "crazy day."

I have to say I don't see Dad make any of the so-called "changes" he vowed he would. Just another broken promise to Mom, but I guess she's used to that by now. Heck, I'm only a kid anyway, what do I know about honesty.. and love and support?

In bed that evening my eyes remain glued to the ceiling. I count the tiles from left to right, up and down, and diagonally too. Every which way you can count them, trust me, I do. That's how I become a great counter, I swear. There's actually an underlying method to my madness. It's not that I savor staying awake half the night and the prospect of waking up all poopy and cranky the next morning. I *have* to keep my eyes open--for one reason...

You must not--cannot--fall asleep, I tell myself. *You have to stay awake in case Mom tries to escape again!* And so I do. Thus begins my sleepless nights; I know deep down in my heart I couldn't bear it if Mom ever left us. I don't want to exist without her in my life! That night, I swear on my Uncle Jim's grave I'll do everything in my power to keep Mom with us. I make it my responsibility to keep the family together. I vow to be the "peacemaker." And so it is...

Why she puts up with my father's wrath, I never understood, though I have my hunches. You see, even as a child, I'm wise beyond my years. Dad is handsome, charismatic, and charming. He knows how to "work" Mom and get what he wants. Fills her head with silly promises of what is to be. Problem is it never lasts because he screws up again. He stays cool and calm for a day or two, and then something sets him off and he goes nuts again, screaming and hollering and taking God's name in vain.

I want to run into the closet and hide behind the jackets and never come out. At least I feel safe there. Dumb, I know, but it's all I can think of to do. As for Dad, I don't believe for a second he harbors evil intentions. He simply doesn't know any better.

So Mom gives in to his misdoings time and time again. It's easier that way, I suppose. Give in, or give up. She holds on for a long time--giving in--until one day I think she just gives up.

Chapter Three
Walking on Eggshells

"I want to go home! I want my own bed!" My seven year-old body is weary. "I want to go to sleep--why can't we leave now?" My siblings, Marilyn, Joanne, Dan, and I plead with our parents, but to no avail. No one listens. No one cares. It's like we're transparent.

The jovial laughs emanating from Aunt Maria's kitchen have grown increasingly louder as afternoon turns into early evening, and early evening transforms into night. The smell of stale Tareyton cigarettes wafts from the kitchen into the living room where we sit and wait, hour after hour after hour.

As much as I adore the fragrant smell of the majestic ocean and the sounds of the babbling seagulls, I am anxious to leave, for we have overstayed our welcome once again. We are more than ready to depart, as this is a scene we have come to know all too well. Let's just say it's etched in our cellular memories.

"When are we going home?" I ask my mother.

"Ask your father," she grumbles.

"Dad, Dad, Dad! We want to go!"

"I'll bid twenty-five in diamonds," he responds. Then "yeah, soon, real soon--now get away!" He takes a huge gulp from his beer bottle. I can tell he's already dismissed me from his thoughts.

I step back, and feel my face grow beet red. I want to scream "let's go you dummies! *Enough* already!" but I wouldn't dare. I know better. I know it's not a good idea to irritate my old man when he's been drinking all afternoon. I know what will happen if I do, so I shrink into the background once again and return to the living room, the jail cell, with the other prisoners.

The night drags on, the laughter escalates to profound insanity, and let's just say the "talk gets cheap." Swear words get slung around like mud in a rainstorm, and our tender ears are exposed to information we should definitely not be hearing. I *despise* it -- *despise it all!*

I begin to get really ticked off and a fury builds inside. We all start to moan and groan gently from the confines of the living room. "We want to go, we want to go..." Our voices drone on and trickle into the party room, but no one answers. Quietly, I march to the outskirts of the kitchen to check out the situation. I pretend to be invisible. Funny though, I don't have to give it a second thought--I *am* invisible.

What I see disgusts me. Miller beer bottles strewn everywhere and the smell of body odor and still burning half-lit cigarettes is enough to gag a maggot. Let's just say it's not a pretty picture.

Definitely not a Kodak moment!

Mom, Dad, Aunt Maria, and Uncle Jack are all acting like jackasses. Their eyes are dark with red stripes through them and their movements appear spasmodic and stupid. Dad struggles out of his chair and wobbles from left to right before steadying himself to a standing position. Weaving to one side of the room and then the other, he eventually finds his way into the bathroom. Upon his return from the can, he whistles and we all jump to attention. Like Pavlov's dogs, we've been conditioned to certain sounds. The whistle means "the party's over, get your asses in the car!" We don't need to be told twice!

The family piles into the light blue Ford Falcon station wagon and we begin our trek home. Dad inches his way onto the main road and suddenly the frivolous mood shifts into stillness. In a blink of an eye all the fun--or whatever grownups call it--is gone. No more howling, no more cracking jokes, no more silliness.

Good! I think, *let's get serious and down to business. Let's get home so us kids can get to bed where we belong...*daylight has given way to an eerie darkness that pervades the air. I nestle against my brother in the way back of the Falcon and anticipate a sleepy ride home. But the ride turns out to be anything but smooth.

What the heck's going on? I wonder as suddenly the road seems rough and bumpy and the car swerves jerkily from one side of the road to the other. *Do we have a flat tire or something?* The car somehow gets back on track again. *Phew, we're okay!* I close my eyes and begin to doze again. Suddenly, my neck snaps forward and back in one swift motion and I awaken with a jolt. *What on earth?*

Then I hear it. There is no mistaking it. My sister Marilyn's voice--loud and clear--yells at the top of her lungs: "Dad, watch out! You're going to crash! We're heading toward the ditch! *Help!*"

I jump up in an instant. I can't believe what I see. I blink my eyes. It's no joke. *Oh, my God!* Dad is behind the steering wheel alright, but his eyes are closed! His body lifeless, his head jiggles from side to side like a puppet. And he's not driving the car!

All I can hear is Joanne screaming "aaaaahhh!" Dan yells "Help! Help! Help! Help!" and Marilyn cries "Dad! Wake up, wake up! *We're going to crash!*"

I grab Dan around the waist, and we hold onto each other for dear life. Without seat belts, we bounce from one side of the car to the other—there's nothing to secure us! My head smashes into the window, *smack!* I'm hurt but ignore the injury as I steady myself back to a sitting position only to find myself slammed against Dan this time.

I kick him in the ribs accidentally and he winces and cries out in distress. I cannot console him! I cannot help him--we are at the mercy of this reckless driver--*our dad!* I smell danger in the air, disgustingly thick, pungent, and toxic. My body shakes uncontrollably due to a dire case of the heebie jeebies. There's no stopping it. I have the chills. I'm nauseous. My underpants and legs feel warm and wet, and I realize I just peed my pants.

My mother finally awakens from her drunken state in the passenger seat.

"John!" she screeches. *"Wake up! Wake up, John! Wake up!* Her voice pierces right through me. Screams are coming from every perimeter of the car now. One sister sobs while the other one yelps like a helpless dog.

"We're gonna die, we're gonna die!" My ears ring, my brain is fuzzy, and my mouth clenches so tightly my lip starts to bleed. I feel like I'm going to pass out. I glance briefly over at Dan. Frozen with terror, he's stiffer than a board and resembles a corpse.

The smell of death surrounds us. It invades our space, it takes over. It grabs us by our throats, stifles our breathing, and set our hearts racing frantically with violent spasms. It pokes gaping holes in our stomachs that make us want to blow dinner. It jabs sharp needles into our skulls—as if we are voodoo dolls—and creates intense fierce compression on our brains. It is relentless and unforgiving. It is pure torture. It is hell! *Oh God, oh God, oh God! Help us, help us, help us!*

Without warning, the Ford Falcon jerks itself back onto the pavement. In a stupor, Dad gazes around as if to say "what happened?" He doesn't have a clue! How queer is that? Ten pairs of eyes remain fixed on the steering wheel for the rest of the wild ride home. Dad graciously remains awake. Won't say alert, but at least his eyes are open. I've never been so glad to pull into my driveway and see the welcome site of home!

Straggling into bed, my mind remains hypervigilant. My body shudders as I yank my bedspread up so high it covers every part of me, including my face and head. I don't want anyone to see...I know what's coming. I feel it waiting to take over. When I sense everyone else is asleep, I let loose and sob uncontrollably for what seems like hours. The tears are for me, my siblings, and for all the children in the world who feel abandoned, rejected, and disrespected. You can imagine I cried a bucket full of tears...

I don't sleep much that night even though my body is beyond exhausted. I can't calm myself down. I need a grownup to hold me and tell me everything will be fine, that this act of stupidity will never, ever, happen again. But no such luck. Just wishful thinking, I reckon. That's a kid for ya...

Alone again in the darkness--it's becoming familiar territory and a place I loathe. And guess what? Not a word is spoken ever again about that wacky night when my family risked serious injury, at the least, and almost died, at the worst. Mum was the word.

Think it's clear that my family is nothing like the Cleavers on *Leave It to Beaver?* Oh no, not by a long shot! Sure, in public everyone thinks our family is *simply smashing.* "Lovely family," I vaguely remember hearing someone say.

What a joke! That couldn't be farther from the truth! *Could they really be talking about us? Come on over and get the real scoop!* I want to tell them, though I know I'd never dare let the cat out of the bag about what actually goes on. Not me! I know better. My sisters and brother do, too. We're really, really good at keeping secrets in my house--especially the one about that night. We walk on eggshells most of the time, cuz we never know when the volcano called "Dad" is going to erupt. Yup, he's quite volatile most of the time. You can't look at him cross-eyed without him screaming and cursing the Lord. That's the norm.

"God ram it!" he'd holler often, and smash his fist onto the kitchen table. When I'd hear those words, I'd run for the hills. Sprint up the stairs faster than a jack rabbit and lock myself in my room. Diving under my bed, I close my eyes tightly, and stuff my fingers in my ears in an attempt to drown out the cacophony. It made me crazy, plum mad, hearing all those dreadful words. They sounded downright dirty.

I hum *Skip To My Lou* over and over again, countless times. I have lots of experience counting in my house. I hum the song repeatedly until the floor beneath me settles and it feels safe to come out again. Could be minutes, could be hours. You just never knew. I didn't like not knowing. Felt odd, left a funny feeling in the pit of my belly. So, I guess you get the drift. Life at the "White House" is pretty darn crazy most of the time. Yup, pretty doggone mad...

Chapter Four
Planting The Seeds

"I *hate* you! I hate *both* of you!" Only eight years old, I can't imagine these awful words are coming out of my mouth, but they do. "I'm going to run away when I get older and never come back! I'm gonna get the heck out of here and go as far away as I possibly can, and you'll never find me! And maybe--*just maybe*--you'll miss me then!"

But I doubt it.

Don't expect a phone call cuz I won't be calling! I think. *Don't bother lookin' for me, either! I don't want to be found--you guys gave up on me a long time ago, so don't even pretend you care! I'll be out of your lives forever! I guess that's what you both want, so good riddance!* In a nutshell, that's often how I feel about my parents and my home life. I'm ashamed to even share this with you.

Don't know if I mentioned this yet, but a little tidbit about me. You know, something no one else knows--unless they ask, or I tell them. You're probably going crazy wondering, so I'll tell ya what it is. I had a really neat imagination as a kid. No, not a *mediocre* imagination, a far out one! I had to, you see, to survive in my zany world. Illusions of grandeur took me to the grooviest places where I could just be *myself* for a while. *Me*--as in a kid! A giddy, quirky, kooky kid. I knew it wasn't real. It was quite foolish you could say, but it felt wicked good at the time.

Like the night I lay in bed, staring at the ceiling tiles once again. I imagine living with another family. I select Nancy Weeks, her three sisters, and her mom and dad. They're a perfect match. I get all goose-bumpy thinking about it. I envision myself in my new home, standing at the edge of the wooden kitchen table, rolling and kneading the Christmas cookie dough. You should see the huge grin on my face--I resemble the Pillsbury Doughboy! There's flour all over my hands, on my chin, even in my hair.

Who cares about the mess? No one in the Weeks' family! I love eating the raw cookie dough. It tastes so sweet and yummy in my tummy. I create festive holiday sleighs, wreaths, and Christmas ornaments, and decorate them with chocolate sprinkles and vanilla frosting. I am in my glory!

Nancy's mom smiles at me radiantly, as she wipes her brow with her red checkered apron, and removes freshly baked cookies from the oven. Her dad snatches a steaming hot cookie off the cookie sheet and pops it into his mouth, quick as a bunny. He "oohs" and "ahs" as the warm, tasty morsel slides down his throat, then licks his lips with delight. He winks at Mrs. Weeks and plants a playful smooch on her cheek. She blushes as the girls and I begin to sing "I Saw Mommy Kissing Santa Claus." It's a magical afternoon, and I couldn't be happier. I feel so carefree and filled with the joy of the season. Life here is good--really, really good!

It's everything I want in a family, truly what my heart desires. As the image fades, I come back to my reality, and ask the same rhetorical question: "Why God? Why can't I have a family like that?" Drifting off and pretending every now and then is sometimes helpful, but not always. I can't escape one true painful fact no matter how hard I try.

The truth of the matter is this: I'm not a boy! That's exactly what my father yearned for. Some things just can't be reckoned with, and this is one of them. How did I know? I had an inkling, a hunch--I knew...a kid just knows some things. Dad wanted a son to whom he could teach all the things his father never taught him, and who he could mold into a prodigy. So he thought, anyway. And guess what? Dad finally got that boy, when my brother Dan was born twenty-one months after me. His ship finally came in, three girls and one miscarriage later...

Dad and Danny go everywhere together. Since dad is passionate about sports and the outdoors, and it becomes his mission in life to help Dan grow and develop into the next Mickey Mantle, Babe Ruth, or some other professional baseball player. Not sure that my brother shares the same passion, but he goes along with it because that's simply the way it was.

I trek along with Dad and Danny to the ball field and am the ball girl. Standing in the outfield for hours fetching balls, deep inside I long to be the one at bat.

"Just one try--just *one*," I say to Pops. "Let me show you what I can do. I can smack that ball right out of the park! Come on dad, give me a shot--please, please?"

"Girls can't hit a baseball," he'd counter. "Come on, son, try again, and swing harder this time. Pat, get a-running. You've got a lot of balls to pick up."

Whether it's baseball, hockey, or another sport, I can't catch a break. Girls can't be athletes in my father's eyes. Needless to say, I never get the opportunity to show him what I have inside of me, who I can potentially be, and how utterly groovy I am. *If only he'd take the time to notice me,* I think. But it wasn't in the cards. Dad isn't able to open his eyes and see his precious daughter. He just can't.

Soon I come to realize I'm not worthy of my father's attention or love, and conclude there must be a defect in me. Why else would he reject me, turn his back on his own flesh and blood? What a disappointment I must be! I began to think I don't like me much either.

My thirst for my parents' attention is insatiable. I long for affection and to hear the words "I love you, sweet child." But I never hear them--not once--from my father's lips. No hugs, no bouncing on Daddy's lap. No piggy back rides to bed. No goodnight kisses--*ever*. I hoped eternally for a happy ending to my story, like in the fairytale stories I read, but alas, I'm not the fairy princess and my story is anything but happy ever after.

Mom does her best to nurture me and my siblings but she lives a fearful existence as well. She falls into a sea of depression which plagues her most of her life. It's all she can do to save herself, never mind her four kids. I continually question my parents' motive for bringing me into this seemingly cruel world. Why couldn't they love wholly this incredible human being standing before them, starving for affection? Wise enough at a tender young age to understand what was missing in my life, but unable to determine how to get it, the question became: Do I keep on trying, or just throw in the towel?

My life is pretty predictable in an unpredictable sort of way. Dad is calm one minute and a raving lunatic the next. Anything or anyone can set him off. Yup, my siblings, my mom, and I witness physical, mental, and verbal abuse on a daily basis. Mark my words--that's a dangerous way to live. Probably like purgatory, I guess.

Slamming doors, screaming, and occasional gut-wrenching

sobs are the sounds I hear before I finally fall asleep at night. I develop a habit of banging my head on my pillow and rocking my body back and forth in an attempt to calm myself down. Sleep is not the norm--my brain has difficulty winding down from such chaotic days. That's how I become a great counter.

When you can't sleep, count sheep, or tiles, or whatever, I tell myself until it seems to become my motto. I count to the trillions easily. I have plenty of time on my hands. All night, every night...

I feel so helpless and powerless when my parents fight. Their constant bickering, cursing, and arguing tear me up inside and have a much greater effect on my psyche than I care to admit. It makes me want to throw up, regurgitate all those frightful feelings swirling around inside. But that doesn't happen, I won't allow it, can't allow it—even when it's more than I can swallow. Thus, here's how I learn to survive in my crazy, everyday world:

I'll be quiet, I'll be quiet--you won't even know I'm here! You won't see me. You won't hear me. I'll stay out of your hair. In fact, you won't even know I exist! My brilliant plan in a nutshell, how to survive in the White residence. Kind of pathetic, when you think about it, huh? I become invisible, try not to exist. I don't know what else to do.

I avoid my dad at all costs and stay out of harm's way so I won't create any more tension in the household. Becoming a ghost is actually quite a huge undertaking. It affects every area of your life. It's particularly hard for teachers and peers to see you when you're a wallflower. I blend in with the scenery so well that I lose my individuality. More importantly, I lose my voice. I find out in the first grade just how far things have gone. A rather "woe is me" story, but I'll share it with you anyway.

I have to go to the bathroom. I need to pee. My hand is up. *Why doesn't Mrs. Wang notice me? What am I gonna do? Should I scream? No, no, I can't--I'm not supposed to speak out loud during a test. But I'm gonna wet my pants if I don't go right now!*

My hand waves back and forth. My eyes plead with her to acknowledge me. She does not. What else is new? *Speak up, you moron! Say something! You're a fool if you don't—what's wrong with you? You're such a weakling...oh no, I can't hold it any longer! It's coming out! Oh, shoot!*

An oddly warm sensation hits me as urine begins to trickle out. Face flushed, I squeeze my thighs together to stop it. *It's no use! Here it comes!* Foul smelling urine drenches the seat of my chair. *Yuck*! I hear it dribble down my seat legs and onto the floor. A big puddle stares up at me. I can't believe this just happened! I want to evaporate into thin air. Every part of my being cringes in agony.

I hate you, Pat! You're a stupid jerk! How are you gonna tell

Mom and Dad this one? You're going to be the laughing stock of the whole school! You'll probably be expelled and no one will want to be your friend anymore! You're in big trouble now. Your butt is gonna get a spanking when you get home!

"Pat wet her pants!" I hear Charles shout. Twenty-three pairs of eyes turn to gawk at me. Mrs. Wang marches over and demands I stand up. I do as she says. I'm a mess. My tights and skirt are soaked. My black patent leather shoes feel all squishy inside from the wet liquid. My body trembles all over and I'm twitching like a neurotic bumble bee. I bite my tongue *hard* to keep from losing it.

My eyes flood with tears and I want to disappear from the classroom, the school--the world! Mortified, I *hate* this--hate it all! *Stop looking at me everyone, please! I already know I'm a stupid failure--a hopeless, miserable, stupid failure!*

Mrs. Wang pages the janitor, who arrives with mop in hand to clean up the mess.

"Would you like to go home and change?" Mrs. Wang asks me.

"Oh, no," I reply without hesitation. I *know* I can't go home. *Dad will give me a darn good lickin' for this one! I'll just sit in my wet clothes for the rest of the afternoon, and Mom and Dad will never find out.* Petrified of my father, I do not desire to feel his hands on me, or the sting of his thick black belt on my butt. When I do receive one of his whoopings, I refuse to let him see the wrath that seethes inside of me.

"Stand still!" Dad would snicker. "Pull your pants down and don't turn around." I'd comply, just as he orders, in a robotic fashion. The crack of the belt against my soft white buttocks leaves me wincing as the pain ravages through my body. *This is inhumane!* I cringe, anticipating the next wallop, for there's never just one whooping.

Oh, Mother Mary, here comes number two! The stinging pain is unbearable! I must be bleeding by now. My heart begins to pump twice its speed, my back stiffens, and my legs become real shaky. My head is swishy and I feel weak all over. *I'm gonna pass out! I can't stay in this body any longer--gotta leave! Peace out...*

But some internal voice kicks in and says *don't give up, Pat! Stay here! Stay in your body. Don't allow him to win!* I desperately want to turn around and spit in his ugly face. I want to punch him right between the eyes and knock his lights out. I *loathe* him--am filled with such hatred! It scares me to think of what I am capable of doing. My thoughts are pure evil. I want nothing more at this moment but for him to experience the shame and humiliation I am feeling. I want to trade places and beat him to a pulp and see how he likes it. Let *him* beg for mercy, but I'd offer him none. I'd just watch him squirm in misery. And like it!

I come back to my senses and realize the inevitable. There is nothing I can do to change things. I am a defenseless victim and must bear this brutality for now. What a gruesome world I live in! My father instructs me to pull up my pants, and go up to my bedroom to think about things.

Think about what? I can't fathom anything a child could do that called for such violence. But I don't dare argue with him or there'd be more beatings. And if that happened, I don't think I'd live long enough to tell you about them. Lying on my bed, hours later, feeling little remorse for what I had done to deserve such abuse, I break down completely. Plain and simple, I lose it. I sob and sob until there are no tears left and all that remains is an empty feeling inside. It's such a lonely, lonely place.

And as far as school goes, I chose to remain in my wet, urine soaked clothes for the rest of the day. Is it uncomfortable? You bet! I could go to the nurse's office and change into a dry set of clothes, but decline that offer as well. I want to punish Pat for being such an idiot, and make her regret this incident for the rest of her life! I can't remotely remember what happens the rest of that Tuesday afternoon in Mrs. Wang's first grade classroom. And you guessed it--my folks never find out about that horrendous day but I carry the mental burden with me always to remember what a nincompoop I made of myself. I set myself up for failure, and the world kindly responded.

Chapter Five
Playtime

Did you ever have a best friend growing up? No, not a person--a *thing*. Something you adored. I surely did, and her name is Corduroy, my very own stuffed animal given to me by my friend Stacy for my 9th birthday. The cutest purple bunny rabbit that ever lived, she's fuzzy and cuddly and so soft. Her ears are big and floppy with a tail white as snow.

Corduroy's my pal and I take her everywhere. What I admire most about Corduroy is her loyalty. Always there for me, through thick and thin, anything goes with Corduroy. Agreeable to whatever I suggest, she never talks back, and I really dig that. We're darn good buddies. Completely trustworthy with my secrets, believe me, she hears them all.

I sing to Corduroy when no one's around. Even though I can't hold a tune to save my life, she seems to really like it. Doesn't mind if I swing her around or throw her up in the air a million times, either. She's a good sport about it all. Sometimes I hug Corduroy so hard I think her stuffing might pop out, but that never happens. Rough and tough on the outside, yet gentle on the inside, Corduroy is my coolest friend and companion.

We have some whopping good times together. I have a picture of us in my Deerskin Trading Post brown leather wallet. I take it out and look at it often, as it's truly a treasure. Probably nine and a half years old in this picture, I'm only a smidgen older than her. Not by much, probably a few months, but I'm still the oldest. I like not being stuck in the middle--just a weird notion of mine.

I get all mushy when I look at this picture of the two of us. Me with my play nurse cap on my head and Corduroy draped in a tangerine paint smock. Sitting quietly at the bottom of my bed, looking up at me with her huge black button eyes, Corduroy's expression is one of pure affection as I tend to her needs. You see, in this particular photo I'm playing nurse and she is my patient. In my imaginary world, Corduroy fell off her Huffy tricycle and got pretty banged up--needed medical attention immediately if I was to save her.

I gather supplies from the emergency kit tucked away neatly in the bathroom medicine chest, and begin fixing her up. I place band-aids gingerly on her knees, scraped in the mishap. There's blood everywhere but I don't flinch. This is no time for a weak gut -- a life is at stake here! I fold a piece of gauze in half, place it gently over her right eye, and tape it to her cheek. She looks better already!

"Don't be scared Corduroy," I murmur to her softly. "You're

going to be as good as new in no time. Just sit still for a few more minutes and we'll be all done. And because you're being such a cooperative patient, I have a surprise for you." Corduroy smiles and winks at me with her left eye—the good one--and allows me to finish my evaluation. I notice her right paw is floppier than usual and determine she has a sprain. This requires rest and immobilization, and I apply an elastic bandage that takes up pretty much her entire paw. I giggle at the sight of her, but only for a brief moment, as I know Corduroy is in no laughing mood. I proceed to place the extremity into a sling and sum up the situation for her.

"All done, my friend!" I exclaim. "You did great—I'm so proud of you!" Then I place a gold star on her forehead, and kiss it with my lips. "This is for being the prize patient of the day, Corduroy! You were extremely brave and now it's time for you to get some much needed rest."

I sweep Corduroy into my arms ever so gently, and bring her close to me. She snuggles her furry head under my chin as her body melts into my chest. I can feel her little heart beating in unison with mine and for a split second it feels like we are one. Who knows, perhaps we are. I know only one thing--that this moment is absolutely perfect. I sing *Rock A Bye Baby* to her for hours while she dozes in and out of consciousness. A rough afternoon, but tomorrow will be a new day--at least for Corduroy. She'll heal quickly, of that I am sure. It brings me such joy to take care of others, especially Corduroy--makes me feel needed and wanted, and fills a void in my life. Makes me feel like you wouldn't believe, like I have a place in the world--like I matter, like I'm a somebody...

Chapter Six
Twisted Dance

Somewhere along the line my daunting task of tending to others' wants and needs takes a mischievous twist of fate. Stuffed animals turn into human beings with raw, untamed emotions-- definitely something I'm not equipped to handle. My goal to remain invisible steers me from my childhood years clear through to adolescence. Considered very shy, I'm basically scared stiff of my own shadow. Petrified to speak up for myself, and intimidated by teachers and peers, I despise being called on in school and suffer great angst when it happens. I don't feel worthy to have an opinion. Heck, I don't feel worthy of life. My self esteem is nil and there isn't much I like about *me*.

I wish I was six inches taller, I'd think. *Why can't I have long, kinky, blonde hair like Margaret? I want to be popular, but I'm such a bore. Why can't I be smart like Holly and Adam? Why can't I excel at anything? Just one thing, Lord, then people might take notice of me!*

Round and round my thoughts spiral as they rummage through my head recycling the same old garbage, day in and day out. Fighting continuous feelings of unworthiness is exhausting. It drains the dang life right out of me. I remain a "good girl" throughout my adolescent years, perform fairly well in school, and don't cause my parents any heartache--at least I get that part right!

Some of my peers begin to experiment with boys, drugs, and alcohol. For the most part I'm not interested, but more than anything I live in fear of the consequences if I were to get caught dabbling with these extracurricular activities.

Makes you wonder if life is even worth living. Sure, I have my incredible imagination to retreat into, but I begin to realize it's only a temporary escape from my painstaking reality. A band-aid won't heal this deep wound beginning to close down my heart.

I do become a whiz--finally excel--at something, though: Stuffing my emotions. *Push those feelings down as fast as you can, Pat! Don't make a peep and you won't get noticed--and in the end, you won't get hurt!* Quite the protective mechanism I devise and, like anything, it has its pitfalls. Big ones, I might add.

The truth of the matter is this: The seeds of my life were planted years before and clearly taking root now. My family and cultural history began to shape my perceptions about who I thought I was--*me*, as in Patty White—a person, with all my thoughts, beliefs, and dreams. I created my own story—exactly who I was in this big, cuckoo world of mine--and it was not pretty and it was not kind. I thought of myself as both a victim and a villain, and believed my life to be bleak and hopeless.

Alas, what does a teenager comprehend at the age of sixteen? I allow myself to get sucked into a vicious game played by adults. In the end, somehow, I always come up with the short end of the straw. In other words, I'm the biggest loser--with a capital "L." One of those special junctures in time—still fresh in my memory, as unfortunately I can't erase it, though I wish I could—began like this:

I bolt upright in bed, jolted out of my sleep. *What's that banging? Who's in the kitchen? What in heaven's name is going on?* I orient myself quickly to the fact that it's one o'clock in the morning, and I'm pretty sure I'm not in Kansas anymore.

"Rita, calm down just a minute--quit slamming the cabinet drawers!" I hear the irritation in my father's voice.

"Get away from me!" my mother yells. "Don't you touch me! You're a dumb-ass, and I can't stand the sight of you!"

"Pipe down, you're gonna wake up the kids," Dad says as he tries to hush her.

"I will *not* calm down! I will *not* be quiet! Quit telling me what to do--you're always telling me what to do and I'm sick of it! You're such a bossy bastard, John White!"

Holy crap, this is serious! I shudder. *What should I do?* I close my eyes tightly for eight seconds and reopen them, hoping this situation will dissipate, but it does not.

"If you don't get out of my face I'm going to puncture your chest with these scissors!" Mom threatens. "Get the hell out of this kitchen! For that matter, why don't you get the hell out of this house?"

I guess my mom means business. Dad scampers up to his bedroom while mom continues to throw stuff around and ramble on about nothing. I hear his bedroom door slam shut as he escapes to his own little world, mumbling obscenities under his breath. I breathe a sigh of relief. Mom can calm down now that Dad has left her alone.

Silently, I pray for peace to return to the house so I can get back to sleep. My eyes close softly as I lay my body back down to rest. My heart rate returns to a normal rhythm and once again I drift off to a more serene place.

This time I awaken to the most foreign sounds, such as I've never heard before. They boggle my mind. I jerk to attention instantly. *What are these noises, and where are they coming from?* I wonder, frightened and feeling very alone. My ears strain to decipher the jibberish I am hearing, but the words don't make sense. Now they become mixed with guttural wails. My body tenses and beads of sweat form on my forehead. My throat narrows and I feel my chest become extremely tight. My heart pounds wildly against my sternum. *Something's gonna break, I can feel it.* My head spins and I don't know what to do. I don't understand what is happening. All I do know is that this house is not safe. I want to hightail it out of this joint, but I can't--I just can't. Something won't let me leave. Something or someone is holding me back...

The sobs coming from the kitchen downstairs get louder and louder. They are cries for help but no one responds--not my dad, and not my brother. I throw on my bathrobe and tiptoe to the top of the stairwell. I peek through the burgundy banister rails and see my mother scrunched up in the fetal position on the living room couch. I catch myself gasping for air, and a queasy feeling overcomes me. *I'm gonna barf any second--I can't believe what I'm seeing!* She resembles a wounded dog about to be put out of its misery. Instinctively, I open my mouth to scream for help, but nothing comes out. I sense impending danger. I can't quite put my finger on it, but something is terribly wrong.

A part of me feels like I am dying with my mother. My eyes well up with tears. Sadness courses through my bloodstream. Perhaps I'll just curl up in a ball and check out now, too. But I don't.

Instead, I race to her side and throw my arms around her. She pulls me awkwardly into her, nearly smothering me in the process.

I don't dare pull away. Her tears splatter all over my face as she mutters a story I can barely comprehend. None of it makes sense. Not to me, anyway. Her words are unrecognizable. They are not of this world. She wails and chokes, and wails and chokes some more. It has a sick rhythm to it. I hold her in my arms in an attempt to console her. I rock her gently back and forth, like a mother comforts her sick child. It's all I can think to do right now. *What is she sobbing about?* I haven't a clue, but I know it is deep stuff. Her sobs of grief penetrate my soul and I absorb it like a sponge. I can feel her agony without a doubt, and it is a lifetime of desperation and trepidation.

When the hysteria subsides, I sit Mom upright gently on the couch. She grabs me tightly once again and yanks me into her chest. I become distinctly aware of how disheveled her silver hair is, and how wrinkled her skin has become. She looks worn out. Just plain tired of living, I guess. Suddenly out of nowhere, Mom lets out a hideous burp and the distinct smell of alcohol spews out of her. The aroma is obnoxious, enough to choke a horse! Mom doesn't bat an eyelash, doesn't even flinch. Nothing seems to faze her.

Slowly everything begins to make sense. I can be naïve at times and a slow learner, but I get this all too clearly now. Mom is drunk! I must be the responsible adult now and take care of her.

But I'm not the adult, I think. I wish my big sisters were here. Why did they have to move out? I can't handle this, it's way too big for me! Shut up, Pat and just do what's right for Mom--quit thinking about yourself for once, and do the respectable thing! What is the right thing? I don't know how to do this--to be a parent! I'm just a kid! Get over yourself...okay, okay, I'll do it...maybe a piping hot cup of tea will help the situation...

Mom looks at me blankly--she's in another time zone. I fill the tea kettle with fresh water from the tap and notice something out of place on the counter. A prescription bottle sits on its side and small white pills lie on the counter everywhere. I scoop up the bottle and read the label. Sure enough, my mother's name is on the bottle and the medication is called Ativan. I know that one by heart. It's Mom's "nerve" pill. I glance at the warning sign, and in bold print I read: *Do not drink alcohol if you have been prescribed this drug. Alcohol can cause increased sedation and somnolence. Potentially harmful if the two are combined.*

"Jesus Christ, what do I do now? I start to panic. *How many cotton-picking pills did she take and how long ago? How much did she have to drink? Dear Lord above!"* I want to wake up my father but I'm reluctant to do so because if she's drunk, so is he and I sense he'll only make matters worse.

My mind begins to speed up. *What if she's overdosed? What if she stops breathing? Should I call nine-one-one now? Oh God, I don't know what to do! Help me, help me*! I peek into the living room to check on her. I'm too obvious. She sees me looking at her and attempts to get up off the couch. Not happening! As soon as she stands up, her legs crumple beneath her. I scurry over and attempt to break her fall. She's absolutely useless. Her body is like Jell-O. Her arms and legs begin to flail in different directions and her head bobbles up and down. I grab her from behind and slide her back down onto the sofa. Finally, she collapses on top of me and I let out a howl. She hasn't a clue what just happened. I shimmy my way out from beneath her. I am pissed. This is not comical.

"Don't move," I say to her. "Stay put and I'll be right back." No response, but at least she's awake. I take that as a good sign. I place the piping hot cup of tea in her lap, and quickly realize that's a big mistake. Mom's hands shake uncontrollably and the tea spills everywhere.

"Damn!" Mom squawks.

"It's okay, Mom. Are you burnt? Don't worry--I'll clean it all up." I jump up to get some paper towels in the kitchen and wipe up the mess. She doesn't seem to be harmed. I'm grateful for the little things. Another cup of tea coming up, but this time I try a different tactic. I hold the cup in my hand and place it up to her lips so she can take little sips. I feel like a mother tending to her baby, and I will do whatever it takes to get her through the night. One milli-second at a time.

I put on the television for distraction, although neither of us is remotely interested. My eyes sting, my body feels wiped, and I have to be up for work in three hours. *Whatever! Quit complaining,* I chastise myself.

Mom's eyes begin to close and I become hopeful. I gaze out the den window into the pitch-black night. The world is silent. All is tranquil, at least for the time being. My eyelids flinch several times and then I finally collapse in sheer exhaustion. A quick nap will do me good. Fat chance, as I am jolted back to reality in no time. Yup, couldn't have been more than a few minutes before Mom's sobs overtake the silence once again. *Here we go--round two! I guess she's got more releasing to do...*

I rub her back, stroke her hair, and hold her hands tightly in mine. I try to tell her she's okay, that she is safe, but the words don't compute. I gaze into her eyes but no one is home. She resembles an alien from another planet, and clearly we don't speak the same language. She is not the mom I know. It is so incredibly hard to watch. On and on it goes, into the wee hours of the morning. I feel like a zombie about now--mentally, physically, and emotionally spent. My ears are shot and my head pulsates with the melancholy sounds that have been playing nonstop all evening. I wonder how my dad and brother have slept through it all.

The cuckoo clock in the kitchen begins to chime. One...two...three...four...five...six chirps. Now six a.m., daylight begins to creep through the window, a welcome sight as I don't feel so deserted anymore. Better yet, Mom has finally passed out. Praise the Lord! I gather her up in my arms and slowly walk her upstairs to her bedroom. She is dead weight and this is not an easy feat. It takes a while but we make it up the stairs, one step at a time. Relieved that she can walk at all, I open the bedroom door and discover the room reeks of alcohol. Go figure. Dad doesn't flinch, doesn't move a muscle. He offers no help whatsoever. I suppose he's feeling pretty darn rotten himself.

I tuck her into bed, clothes and all. Don't care about details at this point. I kiss her on the forehead, whisper "I love you," and softly close the door behind me. In a fog-like state I shuffle to my own bedroom. It is six thirty a.m. and time to get ready for work. I want to call in sick in the worst way, but I can't. Dad would not approve. Besides, I need the money—badly, since I'm trying to save for college and all.

"Six hours is all you have to get through, Pat--then you can come home and take a long nap," I moan to myself. "Okay, okay,

I'll do it." At least things should be quieted down by the time I get home.

I return home from work, wiped out. Plum tuckered out after pulling that all-nighter. Ever hear the saying "don't count your chickens before they're hatched?" Well, I'll tell ya don't, cuz you'll only be disappointed! I was hoping someone would ask how I was. Nope, wrong again! That's precisely what I mean about never getting your hopes up or you'll just be disappointed time and time again.

Mom looks madder than a hatter as she folds laundry at the kitchen table, and hardly acknowledges me. Dad stomps through the kitchen and barely whispers hello.

"What the heck?" I mutter to myself. *I didn't do anything wrong--remember you knuckleheads? It was the two of you who were feuding. Mom, did you forget who took care of you last night? Not your husband, that's for darn sure! It was me, your daughter! Doesn't anyone care about me--my thoughts, my feelings? I guess not!*

Dad attempts to talk to Mom eventually, but she nearly bites his head off. I guess he decides to talk to me instead, and that pisses her off even more. Caught in the middle of their sick game, I don't like it one bit. It feels wrong, it feels evil, and I sense there will be no winner in this game--only losers. Big, big losers, who could lose it all, including their life, if they're not careful. Anyway, that was the first of many all-nighters, if you catch my drift. Just the beginning of what I came to call the "twisted dance" between father, mother, and daughter.

By now you've probably figured out this mother/daughter relationship is a bit odd. You are right on! Mom tells me her troubles and confides to me her insecurities about her marriage as if I was her therapist. I observe her actions, listen to her words, and grow up thinking men are superior to women; that women should be seen and not heard. Apparently, life is meant to be a struggle and just plain hard. I carry this heavy burden at such a young age, but don't know any better.

Much later, I wonder what I'd have been like if our mother/daughter relationship had been different--what if she'd supported and nurtured me, treated me as a teenager and not an adult? Such events lay out the groundwork for how a child will mature into an adult--confident and strong, or submissive and weak. You know exactly which category I fell into...

Chapter Seven
Meeting The Devil

You know how I spoke of my so-called brilliant plan to become invisible in order to survive in my zany, wacky, crazy world? Well, I guess I forgot to mention that this plan wasn't foolproof--oh no, not by a long shot. It backfired on me but good--Holy Toledo, did it ever!

Ever hear the English proverb "better the devil you know than the devil you don't?" The devil I was about to acquaint myself with was a monster--a downright insensitive, mean, scoundrel filled with self-loathing, a bastard who sought justice by inflicting misery and affliction on innocent bystanders. The thought of this cad makes me shudder. I had the pleasure of meeting this wretched dude one steamy, hot summer evening when out on the town with my girlfriends as we cruised down to Salisbury Beach to check out the sights--you know, the guys.

A couple of months back, I'd made a new friend and we became bosom buddies immediately--connected like you can't imagine. Her name? *Alcohol!* Yup, I discovered I love the calming effect booze has on me and how I could feel silly, happy, and oh, so cool. No longer shy or awkward, I experienced a side of me I didn't know existed. I came out of my shell, felt alive for the first time in my life--and I dug this new Pat! Hip and mouthy at times, she kind of liked breaking the rules.

This particular Saturday night we hop into Lola's cherry red Ford Fairlane convertible and off we speed with the tunes a'crankin'. We're hot stuff, seeing as we are sixteen and sophomores in high school. Fired up alright, ready to rock and roll and party the night away, we're wicked pumped. I'm looking forward to a night of fun and frolic, and maybe some smooching to boot! After all, my new motto is "live on the edge...live dangerously and don't get caught in the process!"

This evening the grapefruit mist goes down way too fast. Buzzed one minute and completely trashed the next, I transform from a giggly teenager into a bizarre idiot in sixty minutes. I vaguely remember going on the Himalaya ride at Salisbury Beach, and almost puking up the pizza and fried dough I'd wolfed down. I stagger off the ride with the assistance of Kendra and Moira, as they attempt to hold me up. Sights and sounds become amplified. I suddenly see double of everything and it's wild! Hysterically funny one minute, downright horrifying the next, faces look distorted and creepy. Weirdos stare at me like I'm a pervert or something, and I become agitated.

"Who are you looking at?" I bellow. "How dare you look at

me? You'd better get out of my way, or I'll knock you down! Don't mess with me because I *will* hurt you!" The nasty thoughts keep coming. I try to suppress them, but I swear I can't! My body steams up and feels ready to explode as I sense danger lurking round the next corner. Next, a violent, irrational voice from within takes over and tells me what to do.

This devil, darker than any I could ever have imagined, is ready to pounce on its prey. It wants to cause malicious harm to anyone or anything in its path--to destroy, to kill. Wrath and resentment swarm out of my pores, and I can no longer see straight. So out of control, it's as if I'm possessed. But I'm not. Or am I? Nothing makes sense!

My chest feels lacerated by a sword that cuts every last strand of hope from my heart. Stripped from my being is every shred of goodness I'd tried to cling to so perilously. It's like being slowly and painfully mutilated--and rightfully so. I take my last breath-- my final breath of existence in this world—when the inevitable happens: *I black out!*

Where am I? What the hell happened last night?

"Holy crap, the room is spinning!" I mumble to myself. "Turn off the light--it's blinding me!" Slowly I open one eye and realize I'm in my bed. It's morning and the sun pours in through the window. *How did I get here? What time did I get in? Did I miss curfew? Oh horseshit, I could be in a heap of trouble now! I'll have to tell a big fat lie when Dad interrogates me, because honestly I don't have a clue. Why can't I remember? Think, you dumb ass! You must remember something!* But I can't—it's anything but a good morning.

My head throbs, and there doesn't seem to be one spot on my ugly body that doesn't scream "help!" My mouth thirsts for something cold to drink, to douse the fire inside, but my gut retaliates with a sharp and definitive "no!" I want to lie back down, pull the covers up over my head, and sleep this hangover off for about a week. Maybe even a year! Forget that the entire evening ever happened!

No way, dummy! My thoughts continue to haunt me. *Serves you right for drinking too much last night--you should know better! You can't handle it, you deserve to feel yucky. You're so pathetic! Thought you were so cool last evening, but you know what? You weren't...you're just a pitiful soul—a nobody!*

I remember my explosive feelings, experienced when all those people gawked at me. But what did I do with those feelings? That question plagues me. I play the scenario over and over again in my head, but get stuck in the same exact place each time. It does nothing but make my head ache even more, and I feel even worse. This sucks, big time!

Hysteria sets in and I'm spooked. I don't feel good about this, not one bit, and know I have to call Lola. I need the gaps in the evening to be filled in for me to have some peace of mind! Dialing her number is the easy part. What comes next is the consequence of learning about the despicable behavior that preceded my blackout. As I suspect, it is not pretty.

"Pat," Lola begins, "our gang was beginning to make our way out of the arcade, when we passed a family who seemed to catch your eye. This adorable little boy was enjoying his swirly pink cotton candy, when suddenly out of the blue you raced over to him and ripped it out of his hands!" I felt my knees begin to buckle as Lola continues to give me a blow-by-blow description of the ugly events that followed.

"You then took a huge bite out of it, tossed it to the ground, and stomped on it! His family was stunned, to say the least. We felt humiliated for you! The little guy started to bawl and you began to laugh like a madman. Your eyes were crazed—it was as if you were possessed! It was so irrational and so unlike you, and you showed not one ounce of regret!"

Oh my God, I was downright mean and it was so uncalled for! I couldn't fathom that I was even capable of such an act.

"Then you took off like a bat out of hell, and raced down to the beach. We chased after you, and were finally able to drag you

59

down to the ground. It was like you were in your own little world and we couldn't get through to you. The entire scene was completely surreal! You looked so melancholy, terrified and forlorn ."

I feel like I'd been kicked in the belly and punched in the nose at the same time--like I've had the crap beaten out of me. I want to curl up in a ball and fall off the planet forever...

"We just let you be," Lola continues. "You moaned softly and cried the entire way home. Frankly, it was tough to watch. We got you in your front door, and after that you were on your own. We prayed that you'd make it to your bedroom safe and sound. And yeah, you got in on time--didn't break curfew."

The guilt and shame I carry inside after this incident is beyond words. I can't shake the images Lola painted and I become ill--literally. Sharp pains swell up from deep down in my abdomen and fill my groin with new hatred for myself. Unmerciful, I believe I deserve every ounce of it and then some.

How could I have done something as horrific as this? I wonder. *I love children and all they stand for--purity, innocence, truth, and unconditional love. All the qualities missing from my own childhood!* Still, there's no excuse for this act of violence and I punish myself repeatedly for it. *Bad Pat, unlovable Pat, dishonorable Pat! You're just plain no good and I hate you, hate you, hate you!*

My fun-filled evening had turned into a disastrous night. How could my self-induced pleasure have led to such torment for myself and others? Sure, alcohol allowed me a temporary respite from my day-to-day hell, and I was able to block out the emotional agony I held onto so tightly, but the high was short lived, and the lows not only destructive to myself but to others, too. And that's not remotely okay.

God, I wish there was someone I could talk to--someone who could guide me! Someone who'd take me under their wing, protect me and give me strength. I'm crying out for help, but no one hears me! My parents can't help me. My friends don't understand, and I can't tell them about my screwy family. I can't tell my teachers, either. Who can I tell, God? Who?

I'm so panicked, God, that I'm not gonna make it in this world! That life is gonna swallow me up whole and no one will even notice that I've vanished. Did you know, Lord, I want to be a pediatric nurse one day--I want to help kids get better when they're sick? I want to make them laugh and smile. I want to hold them and tell them everything will be okay. But I'll never become that kind of nurse because I'll never be good enough! I don't know how to be good enough! I don't deserve to be happy and to love someone or something. How can I love others when I can't love me?

What do I know about love and feelings anyway? It's dangerous to feel—it can get you into a lot of trouble, as you can see, Lord. Feeling has gotten me into nothing but mischief. Then I feel guilty, sad, angry, and mad. It's more than I can handle! So, I'll continue to push my feelings down and bury them alive. Not that this plan is working, either--it really isn't but it seems the lesser of the two evils. Maybe I won't get hurt as much!

That's exactly what I do in order to remain recognizable, to not rock the boat. I squelch my emotions and never let anyone see the real me. You might say I have to become a fake to maintain some form of stability in my life, to stay afloat for as long as I can. And most days, believe me, I thought I was sinking.

When you mask feelings, you lose a huge part of yourself. You become inauthentic. You pretend to be someone you're not. How fake is that? I became the very thing I despised. A big, fat, faker! *How pathetic I am...shame on me!* I learn to suppress my anger, sadness, anxiety, and fear. Where it all goes I hadn't a clue, and frankly I don't care, as long as I don't have to *feel*. Feeling is too dreadful. So, I clam up, shut down, and retreat from the real world, basically to survive. It isn't easy, but I do it--I have to.

You're probably wondering if I ever danced with the devil again after that God-awful night at Salisbury Beach. The truth of the matter is vague and ambiguous--I did indeed dance with him again, but not in the usual way. And this particular devil must have had an ounce of goodness in him, for I never harmed a young child again. I swear... The only little one I continued to hurt was my own inner child, and it was a non-stop, ritualistic form of self-abuse, I reckon, and I was quite proficient at it. Don't forget, I was taught by the best, and I had lots and lots of experience...

Chapter Eight
Escape To Nowhere

People wounded early in life often have trouble cultivating intimate relationships. Petrified to show their vulnerable side because their belief system tells them they will only be rejected once again, often they feel like damaged goods.

So what did I know about love and developing a healthy intimate relationship with the male species? You hit the nail on the head: Absolutely nothing! Couldn't even open my mouth to say "hi" to a guy, never mind engage in a deep, meaningful conversation about life. Sure, I daydreamed of being Barbie--and Ken would be my gorgeous date. He'd sweep me off my feet and we'd fall head over heels in love and live happily ever after. Quite the fantasy world, wouldn't ya say? Sure, I desired the real thing, but lacked a few of the main ingredients, namely self love and self worth.

I had lots of crushes on boys my age, but not one of them ever knew. Most of the guys were out of my league anyway. I went for the jocks--the handsome, athletic, outgoing types. Average looking, introverted, and far from athletic, it was a long shot that I'd ever attract that type of guy. I never did, which was a self-fulfilling prophecy, I guess.

I spent my high school years observing, an outsider always looking in. I watched couples as they paraded through the corridors hand-in-hand, giggling and looking all googly-eyed at each other. Life seemed carefree and frivolous, and I secretly desired their lives. In fact, I was quite jealous, as I longed for someone to hold my hand or sneak a kiss onto my cheek. I wanted my knight in shining armor to slip me a love note during science class. Contained in this note would be an invitation to the senior prom. And of course, I'd accept graciously.

I envision us dancing the night away, holding each other ever so close. At the end of the evening he says: "Pat, you're my girl," and I melt into his arms. We become inseparable and life is blissful. After all, isn't that how Romeo and Juliet came to be? Why couldn't I experience that type of romantic love? Oh, I forgot for one brief moment that I am a *reject*--how could I be so stupid? Sorry, for my forgetfulness!

I do have one steady relationship when I'm about to enter college. Kipp is cute, ambitious, and genuinely a nice guy. I fall for him instantly, and we have definite chemistry together. We date off and on for three years, though mostly off, as Kipp seems to fancy hooking up with chicks from his college town. The few times he comes home for a visit, he gives me a jingle and I drop everything to see him.

What a sucker! I let myself be emotionally abused by a guy who isn't ready to be with me only. He wants to have his cake and eat it too, and I'm willing to settle for that. I feel sad more than happy in the relationship, but I refuse to let go. Stubborn old girl, I am. As pathetic as it sounds, some part of me is used to being abused and I accept it. I allow him to penetrate my heart and he does just what I'm accustomed to--he breaks it, shatters it into a bazillion pieces. I feel unlovable and unworthy big time. Same theme, different day. Reckon it isn't all his fault either; it takes two to tango. We're simply doing different dances!

My story continues and the daily dialogue of "you're just not worth it, Pat, no one will ever love you," keeps playing in my head. It's enough to make me want to exit this world. Honestly, there are days when I'm ready to hang it all up. Throw in the towel. Check out for good. The possibility of ending my suffering is actually quite appealing. My spirit can't take much more. Life is simply too much to handle--until I meet Todd...

Todd sought me out--comes after me big time. I'm not interested in him in the least--after all, he's three years younger. He's a *baby*. He's not my type, so I think, yet I'm bedazzled by his attentiveness. No guy has ever been so enamored with *moi*, and it scares the heck out of me. I ignore his phone calls and steer clear of our common hangout spots. Todd is ruthless in his pursuit. He damn near wears me out until I finally agree to one date. After consulting my mother and sister, I figure I'll get a free dinner out of him and nothing more.

Only one problem--he wants more. Just a kiss, but I'm not up for that. I'm not feeling him, if you catch my drift--I'd rather kiss the Blarney Stone. Somehow, I make it through that first date and vow there will be no more...but I'm way off base.

Still can't figure out quite what happened, but within a few short months, Todd and I are going strong--hot and heavy in love, I might add. Todd is a fabulous teacher and I his star pupil. Witty, charming, and ever so patient with me, he teaches me all about the birds and the bees, and I must admit I'm a fast learner! Things move quickly, and before I know it we're exclusive. It's a whirlwind relationship, the kind I dreamed about. It's everything I ever wanted. My fairytale is coming true--or is it?

JOURNAL ENTRY: 10/7/80, 2:37 a.m.

My Dearest Todd:

I've finally found someone who adores me! Your love is genuine and pure. When I look into your baby blues, I lose myself completely. I get all soft and mushy inside. When I hear your voice on the phone, chills start racing through my body. It's like every atom of my being is charged with your energy. It invigorates and rattles me at the same time. When you caress my cheek I become putty in your hands.

Nothing, no one else, matters. It's as if we are the only two people left on earth. And when you kiss my lips, my heart begins to throb. It swells with love and passion for you as the wall I have built around it begins to melt away.

No one has ever been able to penetrate this wall, Todd, until you waltzed into my life. I can feel your presence as you enter a room. I smell you, taste you, breathe you. I've never experienced this kind of love in my life. I have to pinch myself at times to see if this is the real deal. And by golly, it is! I still can't believe you found me. It's both astonishing and utterly crazy.

But, there's a part of me that believes I don't deserve you, Todd. I've never been worthy of a man's affection, so why should you be any different? Once you get to know the real me, your undying love will fade away. You'll see me for who I truly am, and you won't like me. That's just the way it is--just the way it's always been. The bottom line, Todd, is I don't believe I'm meant to find true love. It's just not in the cards. Never has been. Men I love always leave. You will, too.

I won't--can't--allow myself to be rejected again. It's simply too caustic. Besides, I've told you about my nutty family, and the last thing I want to do is drag you into my chaos. That wouldn't be fair and I have way too much respect for you. I think it would be best if we stop seeing each other. That way, you can move on to find a girl who'll fulfill your dreams. I wish you nothing but the best, Todd. You deserve nothing less.

Always,
Pat

My heart feels like it's breaking in two, severed in half with a machete. It hurts real bad. I can't stop crying, and Mom starts asking questions. I can't tell her the truth though, since she's part of the reason I end the relationship. I don't want to worry her. I do what has to be done. How can I trust that Todd will love only me and not run away? I can't take that chance. I have to let the best thing that's ever come along go. I have to send him away before he rejects me. Attack the attacker before he digs his claws in deep and destroys me. Sick thinking, you might say, but that's how my mind works. Always have to be one up!

Todd--romantic that he is--refuses to end our relationship! In fact, he's downright furious that I doubt him at all. He doesn't leave me, either. Instead, he asks Mom and Dad for my hand in marriage. Yup, you guessed it--Todd proposes! My parents couldn't have been happier. I, on the other hand, feel quite ambivalent.

I love Todd without a doubt, and there's a huge part of me that wants to escape the hell hole in which I live--to get away from the abuse forever. But there's a bigger piece of me that's unsure about leaving my mom. Who'll tend to her needs when she goes over the edge? Who'll comfort her? I've come to understand that her whole world revolves around me. It's glum, but I'm her life. Can she live without me? I, for one, don't want to be the cause of her demise. She's been hurt enough. I may have to stick around to keep the peace in the "White House." If that's what's necessary,

I'll do it, no questions asked. It's my duty and obligation as a daughter.

Ultimately, my heart chooses to marry Todd. Too good and too kind to pass up--a gift from God!--I'm not about to lose the best person who's ever entered my life. However, I fail to comprehend that getting married won't solve a darn thing, as far as leaving my troubles behind. In reality, it's an escape to nowhere.

Don't know if you're aware, but chaos and family problems travel. Yup, doesn't matter how far across the continent you go, your shit comes with you--at no extra charge! Our wedding and honeymoon are sensational, yet Mom is always on the back burner. I can't stop thinking about her and how she's doing. Is she melancholy? Is she lonely? Is she safe? Does she need me? Sick, I know, but that's the crux of my situation. My family and me—we're a package deal...

You can see how easily I carried my family drama into my new marriage. A huge mistake--gigantic!--I can't figure out how to separate the two worlds. Furthermore, my unfinished business comes along, too. You know, those distorted beliefs and emotions I've repressed. They percolate just beneath the surface, waiting for the opportune time to come out and play. Being young and unworldly is probably a good thing, because if Todd knew what our future held, he probably would've run for the hills! I wouldn't have blamed him one bit. My family *stuff* was way more than Todd probably ever bargained for and--believe me--the fun and games were just beginning.

The name of this dangerous game is called co-dependency, and I'm the key player--the *co-dependent*.

Chapter Nine
The White Picket Fence

I believed it was every girl's dream to be happily married, live in the cottage with the white picket fence, and have lots of babies with which to cuddle and coo. You know, like the *Sound of Music*--everyday a play-day filled with adventure and oodles and oodles of fun with Mama and Papa...

You're probably thinking: What planet is she from? Call it a delusion, perhaps a psychotic episode, but that's my "perfect family" fantasy. The never-ending dreamer--that's me!

Todd and I talk about having kiddos all right. He's twenty, I'm twenty-three when we get hitched, and we both think waiting five years is the best route to go. That way we'll save some money, establish ourselves in our respective careers, and enjoy our honeymoon period. You know, get to know each other as husband and wife. We're young kids ourselves in many ways, so it makes sense to give our relationship time to grow. Wait five years and *then* have six kids--that's our pre-baby pact.

Somehow we get the sequencing backwards and only two weeks into the marriage I find myself nauseous, dog tired, and a wee bit cantankerous. I can't keep down a stitch of food. Holy smokes, Pat is pregnant! So much for the honeymoon! So much for our plan...

Colleen arrives nine months later and, at nine pounds one ounce, she's a bright bundle of joy. I'm over-the-top excited to take her home from the hospital and play house with her and Todd, just as I'd fantasized. But things don't go quite as expected. Todd sprains his ankle the night before my discharge and, hobbling around on crutches, it's all he can do to fend for himself.

"No problem, I can handle this," I mumble to myself. Boy, am I in for a rude awakening! Despite having given birth to a baby, nothing--and I mean *nothing*—has prepared me for motherhood! Don't get me wrong, childbirth is one of the most intoxicating experiences I've ever had, but the care of a newborn is monumental – and 24/7!

I give Colleen her three a.m. feeding our first night home. *This is simple--piece of cake!* I think. With that, as if on cue, Colleen lets out a huge burp and vomits her entire feeding down my back and all over the mahogany rocking chair. Simultaneously, she soaks my nightgown with urine and, just for good measure, smelly brown poop. She'd let go from every orifice possible. Welcome to motherhood!

Nope, not quite what I expected! I tend to Colleen, then Todd, and finally, to *me*. It's a ton of work. Being a mom is beautiful, yet exhausting. I want to be the perfect mommy and wife. I want to get it right and for sure do not want to fail. Thank God, Todd is nothing like Dad! He's an amiable, loving, and determined young man. The downside is that he puts in a ton of hours at his family business. Needless to say, we are saving up to buy a place of our own.

I work full time as a nurse at a local hospital as well - our lives are busy and full. Six months later, *oops - Pat's pregnant again!* We *can't* stick to our original plan. Never was very good at calculations...

Baby number two, Erin, nearly an Irish twin, weighs in at seven pounds, eleven ounces. We welcome her into the family with open arms. She's a delight, just like her sister. Two babies present a wee bit more of a challenge, which in turn strains our relationship. At the end of the day there's little to no "Pat and Todd" time—we're both physically and mentally worn out. I take care of patients, infants, my husband, and myself, and Todd now works two jobs to make ends meet, including weekends. This minimizes our time alone even more, and leaves me feeling anxious and resentful. There's never enough time!

Communicating our individual needs had never been a priority until now, and Todd and I lack knowledge in this area. I don't know how to assert myself, which complicates matters and frustrates the hell out of him. All he has to do is raise his voice, even a decimal, and I shut down. It's too familiar, too close to home, and not good, so I retreat to the only place I know that feels a little safe: Within.

Thankfully, our spats never last long, as we share a truly passionate love for one another. A mutual respect, you might say. Heated arguments turn to lust and passionate lovemaking in the bedroom, where all is forgotten, at least for the time being. Probably not the remedy a shrink would recommend, but it suffices. Very well may be how our third kiddo, Patrick, is conceived two years later.

At nine pounds, four ounces, Patrick is two weeks overdue and appears to have no desire to venture out into this world. In hindsight, perhaps he knows far more than the rest of us! Popping him out is no easy feat, but well worth it! A welcome addition to the Bateson family, fuzzy-headed orange hair, chocolate brown eyes, and all. He is stunning!

We feel so blessed! Our cups and our hands are full with three amazingly gifted souls! Three cherubs in less than four years--our max! It's a no brainer...has my picture-perfect world finally arrived? Can it be that all of the melodrama and pandemonium is now really a thing of the past, a piece of history? I surely hope so...

Chapter Ten
Motherhood

Telling my children I love them is a priority, I guess, because I didn't grow up hearing those words and feel destined to do things differently from my parents. I so want to excel at being a great mom cuz there's no "do over" here! I never excelled at anything before, and know I'll get only one shot. This is my golden opportunity to prove myself!

Forever looking outside myself for answers, doubting my abilities, and seeking Todd's approval only puts more pressure on me. I want desperately to be recognized and validated, but I judge myself constantly: *Am I honorable enough? Am I worthy enough? Can I be a really superb mom and wife? Can I--for once in my life!-- get something friggin' right?* I'm sure you're as exhausted as I am listening to all this chatter rumble round and round in my head.

I can't control my zany inner world, but can for sure control my outer one. At least, I *think* I can. My home--spotless, neat as a pin, and in perfect order--feels safe and stable, and I like it that way. Don't like clutter, hate messes—they make me feel as if I'm on shaky ground. I run a tight ship, too, if I do say so myself! My spic and span kids--must have shiny kids to go with the squeaky clean house—guard me from worrying about what others think of me and my kin. Here I am, trying to keep up, still trying to find myself--and it's oh so unbearably draining...

Entertaining is definitely not up my alley. In fact, I plain suck at it--don't know how to do it, how to be the hostess with the most-ess. Growing up, most family gatherings in the White House were quite topsy-turvy, so I suspect it's fated that my social events be a bit tumultuous, too. Monkey see, monkey do.

OK, so I'm trying to pass the buck, trying to put the blame elsewhere, instead of precisely where it should be--on me. I fuck up royally once again--yeah, big time! The scene is Patrick's christening day, and my inner critic--an uninvited guest--decides to make an appearance. Sit tight and proceed with caution; here are the details of that unforgettable day from hell:

I recollect feeling so out of balance that infamous Sunday afternoon in September. Totally worn out, a newborn and two toddlers in tow, a menstruating bloody mess (no pun intended!) it's my missing wedding ring that sends me into a tailspin and pushes me over the edge. What follows this day goes completely downhill from here—I'm way, way out of whack...

Imagine the scene: Kids crying, Todd screaming "we're gonna be late for church!" and I'm literally in my own world pacing the cage, thinking *how can I escape, jump ship, abandon my crew?*

These and other poisoned thoughts flicker through my mind. *I just can't seem to get this right, I can't do this! Maybe I'm not cut out for motherhood!* Meanwhile, my inner critic pipes up, and says *shut the hell up and get your no-good keister in the car!*

Those dreaded words "get your ass in the car!" stir up old memories, and for a split second my father's angry face appears in front of me before it bursts into flames. Intense rage seeps out of my skin, and a twisted knot forms in my belly and courses its way up to my throat. I want to dislodge it, spew it clear across the room, but it stays stuck right where it is. Tightly restricting, it chokes me! An explosion of some sort appears imminent...

The toot of the car horn jolts me back to reality. *What the hell just happened?* I wonder. *Who am I--Dr. Jekyl and Mr. Hyde?* Soaked with perspiration, I throw water on my face, crack that half-assed bogus smile of mine, and head out the door. No one ever has to know what just happened--I'll tuck it away in that safe hiding place of mine. That familiar cold shiver rivets up my spine, and I know it's an ominous sign...

I must say, the party goes smashingly well up until dessert time—that's when all hell breaks loose...

"Honey, can you get me a cup of coffee?" Todd inquires from the living room.

"Sure thing," I answer, "coming right up!"

Todd swings his arm around to grab the cup from behind and the boiling hot liquid spills all over him, the brand new leather sofa, and the rose carpet.

"Jesus Christ! What did you do that for?" he responds angrily and glares at me. If looks could kill, I'd be a dead woman about now, but as usual, I say nothing. All eyes turn to me. I'm totally flabbergasted. Flashback: Mrs. Wang's first grade class! I'm six years old all over again! This wound reopens instantly and something deep is triggered. Shame and guilt invade my adult body as I run upstairs, slam the bathroom door, and ball my eyes out.

"Prick head!" I say as I look at my reflection in the mirror. Ticked off at both myself and Todd, I know I must return to the party, though that's the last thing I want to do. I much prefer to hide out alone. Who'd notice I was missing, anyway?

I return to the kitchen to join the women folk, and know they can see the distress on my face.

"Pat, do you want a cold drink?" asks one guest.

"A cup of coffee or tea?" queries another.

"I'll have a shot and a beer!"I hear myself answer abruptly. I don't even know where that thought comes from--I only know I don't think twice about it. Seagram's Seven whiskey goes down real smooth. Burns my throat but settles my stomach and nerves almost instantly. Takes the edge off, dulls the affliction, lessens my burden.

"I'll have another!" I blurt. The second shot is as delectable as the first. Still smooth and refreshing, my insides tingle. The beer follows the whiskey—simply the chaser, as my dad would say.

My body begins to loosen up and relax, but unfortunately that includes my tongue. Odd thoughts pop into my head. I try to shrug them off. Faces start to get a little fuzzy, voices sound hyper-exaggerated and, suffice it to say, the show is about to begin.

I recollect staring intently at my mother-in-law, who's sitting beside me at the kitchen counter. Always exquisitely dressed, red hair coiffed just so, Mary resembles a porcelain doll. Strict, stern, yet loving, she intimidates me. She roars like a lion; I whisper like a lamb. She speaks her mind; I do not. Thus, our relationship sometimes resembles oil and water and we don't always mix well.

She now becomes my focal point of the afternoon, for whatever reason. Impeccable timing, as always, I decide to come out of my shell and assert myself. I butt in on her existing conversation to inquire: "Mary, do you hoot and holler when you have sex?"

I get no response. My mother-in-law doesn't even bat an eyelash, doesn't flinch. Not what I was hoping for. The devil in me despises inattentiveness, so I raise my voice an octave higher and rudely interrupt her once again.

"I *said* do you hoot and holler when you have sex?"

Mary hears me this time--loud and clear—and so does every other female in the kitchen. Her face turns ghostly white as if she's just seen a demon, and her mouth drops open, clearly with embarrassment at the question I keep jabbing at her. I hear snickers in the background, and the kind of nervous laughter that occurs when someone says something totally inappropriate. I dismiss the frivolity my sisters-in-law Laurie, Tammy, and Maureen attempt to bring to the situation and continue to peer intently at Mary.

I want an answer--*I want it now!*--and she's not giving it to me! It's clear she is mortified--dumbfounded beyond belief. I glare at her one more time and, without a second thought, get up and leave the room. *No answer? I'm outta here!* Party's over for Pat! What a terrific hostess I am.

I hightail it out of the kitchen and head upstairs to Patrick's bedroom to check on him--at least I think I do. It's all hearsay, as I have no recollection of the rest of the evening, even though the night was still young. My sister-in-law Maureen comes looking for me, and finds me sprawled out on the carpet like Jesus Christ on the cross. I must have been checking on my son, as any devoted mother would, and passed out cold. Even in my stupor, I still tended my flock, trying desperately to be the "perfect" mom...

You can imagine the harassment I receive from the family after this shenanigan--all purely self-inflicted! I deserve it all, every bit of it. Talk about being taken down a peg or two. Humiliated now that the cat's out of the bag--they'd never seen this side of Pat before! My mother-in-law accepts my apology easily; she isn't angry with me, just shocked at what had come out of my mouth. It was a slip of the tongue, nothing more...*yeah, right!*

My deeply wounded inner child, so helpless and defenseless, tried to come out to play but instead wreaked havoc on those she loves. It's beginning to be quite a challenge to tame this bitch! She can be ruthless and likes to win at all costs, even if the price is an innocent bystander.

Who is this beast inside of me? What does she want? What does she need? Heck if I know! So much for celebrations and parties, I guess I'm simply carrying on the White family tradition of throwing some of the most entertaining, eye-opening parties ever. Though not something to be proud of, I am--for sure--pretty darn good at it!

Chapter Eleven
Gone But Not Forgotten

Juggling two families can be pretty darn tricky. When at Mom and Dad's house attempting to extinguish fires, I experience tremendous guilt for abandoning my children and husband. Despite my remorse, however, when the home phone rings, I'm off and running--don't want to look like the neglectful daughter! But, as we all know, looks can be deceiving...

My folks say "jump!" and I ask "how high?" I think I can fix them, make them happy. I give them all of me, but it's never enough. They're like my secret addiction. I always want more approval, and can't get them out of my head. Some days I can't catch my breath, and feel frazzled to the max. Perhaps I'm heading for the loony bin myself. *What have I gotten myself into? How did I ever get here?* I feel like I'm on the hamster treadmill racing at a hundred miles per hour, destination nowhere.

Yet after each escapade Mom and Dad's lives return to normal, while I remain on high spin of the wash cycle, unable to stop the incessant bedlam and anarchy that churn within. My stress level shoots through the roof as my resentment rises. Who cares? Not them!

The Pollyanna in me wants to believe they'll change, that something good will come of this, but it is pure fantasy. When did pleasing everyone become so complicated? *What about me and my desires? When did I lose me? Better yet, had I ever found me? Had I ever been a top priority in my own life?*

I see the look in Todd's eyes. He says nothing--he doesn't want to rock the boat, but he's annoyed with all the shenanigans. He pays while I play this sick game. Honestly, I really did try to keep my two worlds separate--but matters got way out of hand somewhere along this path called life.

At a family member's suggestion, I seek out a therapist, a family counselor. Our first meeting necessitates lots of tissues.

"Tell me about your childhood," she says.

"Have you got about a year?" I mumble. The words pour out of me, I never realized how much I have to say, how much emotion is pent up inside. It's a freeing feeling, yet there's a side of me that fears I am a tattletale. *I'm squealing on my own flesh and blood! What kind of a daughter would do that?*

"What's in it for you?" inquires Amy, the therapist. "Clearly you must be getting something out of this relationship or you wouldn't be in it."

To be honest, the thought had never crossed my mind. No one ever asked me that question before: *What's in it for Pat?* For sure I got attention from my parents for being at their beck and call. It's my M.O.--Pat the "helper," and I take great pride in that. It gives me an identity. Kudos to me, look at me, aren't I special? I can see myself up on the pedestal, both of them cheering and applauding my endeavors. There's a sense of empowerment in this love-hate relationship of ours. *Obviously* I'm getting something in return.

"Is it worth it?" Amy continues to probe.

Stumped, I have no response to her thought-provoking question. Suddenly this conversation doesn't feel so pleasant anymore. Amy suggests I detach from the relationship with my parents.

"Loosen the reins a little," she says. "You must let go."

Just hearing this makes me squirm. More tissues--pronto!

"I can't do that," I protest.

"You must," Amy states, "otherwise the situation will only get worse. The older they get, the more dependent they'll become. Are you prepared to care for two geriatric parents? God help you, if you agree to this! And, believe it or not Pat, if you say no, they *will* survive without you."

"No they won't," I murmur under my breath. I don't like what she's telling me. *She doesn't understand us, she doesn't have a clue about our family dynamics,* I convince myself.

Amy recommends I keep a journal where I can write my

thoughts and feelings regarding Mom and Dad. She says it's a great release. Don't know what she means, but I'm open to it. I attempt to stay objective and see her side of things; she is the expert, you know.

"I have a fabulous book I suggest you read," she adds. *Codependent No More*, by Melody Beattie—it'll shed some light on what you're going through and assist you to move forward in your life with your husband and kids. For that is where you belong."

But what about Rita and John?, that old proverbial voice squeals from within. *Shut up, Pat, and shake her hand. The session is over.*

Leaving Amy's office I feel ambivalent, yet lighter. Still, a sense of betrayal washes over me--I am a traitor. Yet for the first time ever, it feels like I have been heard, that somebody out there cares enough to listen and gets the ever so complicated *me*.

Putting down Melody Beattie's book proves nearly impossible. The hairs stand up on my arms as I read the signs of a codependent. It's like she's speaking directly to me, it depicts my life to a "T." How crazy that there is a name for this madness, this peculiar world I have come to know and loathe. I'm a *codependent*--an enabler—and I never knew! All these years...all those lies, all this drama! *This* is what it's called! It all becomes clear as I understand also that codependency followed me into my own marriage. This huge web of evil and deception moved right into my own home--what a bloodcurdling thought!

Question is can I let go and stop trying to fix and control my parents' destiny? Perhaps this is the biggest pitfall of all, and the reason I'm so reluctant to exit this toxic relationship. In my wildest dreams, I always hoped there would be "a happily ever after" ending to our story.

Is it time now to sever the umbilical cord, to pursue separate paths? It all seems so realistic in the book, but books are often full of trickery, meant for everyone except me. I must let this information sink in, and digest it and see what the future holds. It's way too soon to tell...

I decide to give journaling a go, and my journal quickly becomes a dear confidante as I disclose anything and everything there. It never betrays me, kind of like Corduroy. Words spill effortlessly onto my journal pages. I'm astounded at all I've held hostage within, undeniably a lifetime of despondence, remorse, and hunger that's lain dormant in the core of my soul. This is virgin territory; never have I entered this space and frankly it's rather intimidating. But also refreshingly titillating; I'm in a safe haven where nothing and no one can hurt me. I can slow down from life's hectic pace and breathe, even if only for five minutes-- I'll take any respite I can get. Maybe, just maybe, my therapist is on to something. Dare I think my ship may be coming in?

Reading becomes my ally, and it's through my dear friend Cheryl I am introduced to the book *Angelspeake,* a new age work about angels written by Barbara Mark and Trudy Griswold. Sisters, they share their experiences and knowledge about how to connect with angels and why one would even want to do so. Basically, they say angels are present in our lives to guide and uplift us on our earthly journeys. They love us unconditionally and want only the best for us.

A dreamer, I've always adored halos, angel wings, and cherubs as a child, and so am totally open to communicating with their world. I'd be still, close my eyes, and invoke the presence of an angel simply by asking and then await a message. Sometimes it would come in the form of whispered words in my ear, others as a hunch or a gut feeling in my belly. Wow, it really is that simple!

Angels are messengers of the divine, that's the long and the short of it, and there is absolutely nothing we can ever do to change their unconditional love for us. I like that, it's just what I need! Although my heart is weighed down with skepticism and suspicion, I go totally out on a limb and find that trusting and believing prove fruitful. I begin to fall head over heels for my new support team! They're unbiased and non-judgmental, available at any given moment to provide assistance, and the only requirement is that I ask and then listen. For sure I can do that!

Committing to "letting go" one itsy bitsy step at a time doesn't come easy, but life is looking up and I begin to assert myself in tiny increments. I choose to care "about" not care "for" Rita and John, and to learn the monumental difference between the two. I'm resigning my role as the enabler! I'll always be there for them, just not in the way I had been before. I swear that life will be very different from now on...

Perhaps it's my angel Thomas who really gets my knickers in a twist when he mutters in my ear "you gotta be nuts!" after I sit week after week between Dad and Mom at their psychologist's office. What the heck am I thinking? *Me,* in the middle of the two of them at a God damned shrink's office because they can't be cordial to each other, listening to their tainted sex lives (or lack thereof), and their other tales of woe. It's *so* pathetic. I *must* be nuts--somebody slap some sense into me!

I try to ease my way out, make myself unavailable when Dad surfaces at my front door crying wolf about Mom, or when Mom asks me to accompany her to a divorce lawyer behind Dad's back. I fret that I'll be shot in he head and left for dead, if he ever finds out about that one! Nightmares include my family finding me buried alive somewhere for my horrible misdeeds. How I hate this game—the stakes are getting too high! But wait, it gets better...

FIREWALK

Todd and I escape to Cape Cod for a "getaway weekend." Bingo, you got it, to get away from the folks. We need some alone time to save our marriage and our sanity. Rest, relaxation, and reconnecting are at the top of the list and thankfully we decompress and manage to unwind. Just what the doctor ordered! I come back rejuvenated and ready to take on the world.

Upon our return home I can't believe my eyes when I find Mom and my sister Marilyn sitting at my kitchen table! Mom is mental, bawling her eyes out. She's run away--again! *What the hell are they doing here?* I wonder. *Why, dear God, why does she have to come to my house? Can't she go somewhere else for a change?*

Todd is speechless, but what can he say? He never intervenes. But, oh the look on his face! I'm ready to hit the skids, go to pieces —this is bullshit! But, as always, there are fireworks to go with the show that never fail to sidetrack me. Dad is berserk on the phone; there's no consoling him, either. By the way, is anyone interested in hearing about our getaway weekend? Guess not, welcome back to the bedlam!

This is the straw that breaks the camel's back. I see stars and the color red. No, not as in the American flag—as in seething rage! They've crossed the line one too many times and this is the tipping point—I'm done playing this corrupted, putrid game! Finally, *I get it*--if I don't estrange myself from this sick triangular relationship and set up some boundaries *asap*, I'll lose everything, including my husband, children, and--last but not least--*me!*

This incident takes it to a whole new level. Todd, who's never said a bad word about my folks, now gets increasingly frustrated at me for not having a backbone. But what can I do? I tried--it was my responsibility, but I failed. He can't get me out of this mess and sadly I know that he can't save me. *Is he going to bolt out of this marriage and leave me? If he does, I can't say I'd blame him, but if he leaves me, what the heck will I do then?*

I think long and hard about it. I contemplate it from every angle possible. Who might get hurt, how much, and for how long. Then tell myself *fuck it, fuck it all! I've been battered long enough and I'm doing this for me!* My insides convulse as I write what I want, what I need. It feels so foreign, writing about me. But I have to do it--I *have* to take charge.

You're probably wondering what I wrote, so I'll share with you my letter:

Dear Mom and Dad:

I think I've been the best daughter I could be. I've been there for you both through thick and thin and tried to take care of and accommodate you always. I thought I could make you guys happy, bring you joy, but your joy is fleeting—it doesn't last and it never will. Bottom line: I cannot fix either one of you, or save your relationship!

Only the two of you, together, can do that--if you choose....

All of this has come at a very high price, and has cost me a lot. I don't know if you're even aware of it, but the three of us and our dependency issue have deeply affected my relationship with Todd and the kids, and I realize now—it's blatantly clear--that they must come first.

You've always been the very best grandparents to Colleen, Erin, and Patrick, and it's of the utmost importance that you know that. They love you dearly and think the world of you both, as they should. I do not want their image of you to change, for that is their reality and their truth. But this isn't about them, it's about us three. I need to step away from the relationship and let you live your own lives. I need to take care of myself and make me a priority.

I don't have the foggiest notion how to do that, but I will figure it out. So I request the following: Please, no more calls when the shit hits the fan! And please don't come by the house several times a day when the turmoil begins and expect me to come running. I won't be available. Call me with some good news for a change, and definitely don't call in the middle of the night! Pat is no longer on the night shift--her duties have ended.

I hope you can understand this and give me my space. I want only the best for both of you, always have. It's time now for Pat.

Always,
Pat

Finally, I said my piece! I seal the envelope, and off it goes. I poured my heart and soul out to them, and it feels splendid! Now I pray they will comprehend. Asserting myself and standing my ground doesn't come easy, but I give it my best shot. Sometimes that's all one can do. The little girl inside of me is very proud of big Pat.

Three days elapse and I hear nothing from Rita and John. Hate to be a pessimist, but this is very odd behavior and extremely uncharacteristic of them. Dad is a man of many words, as you know, some of which I care not to repeat.

On day four, the phone jingles and I jump with enthusiastic anticipation to answer it. Dad is on the other end of the receiver. Call it intuition or that angelic gut feeling, but suddenly I tense up. When I hear his voice I feel frozen in time, just like that! *Is he going to grab me through the phone and whack my behind, or send me to bed without dinner?* Either option threatens me and I feel irrelevant and microscopic once again.

"Pat, your mother and I received your letter," he informs me.

Thank goodness, the worst is over! At least that's what I presume.

"We don't understand what you're trying to say," he continues. "What's this about you and your needs? We've always been there for you! And what have we ever asked for in return?"

On and on he went. Speechless, no--plum bamboozled—I wonder if I'd written my letter in Spanish! I could understand they might be in denial at first, but seriously, there was no mistaking my words--they couldn't have been more exact and precise, and they were in God damned English! I can't get any clearer than that, you lame brains!

While it was the God's honest truth they'd been there for me, it was clear the return button was stuck on them, and the stakes were now way too high. Enough of this jaded game we always play! I don't want to jeopardize my mental and emotional well-being any longer!

The conversation goes nowhere fast. I need to hang up so I can bang my head against the wall. What an idiotic idea my letter had been! It totally backfired in my face and, unfortunately, I have no backup plan.

The phone falls silent after this epic event, as do my parents' voices. It's as if they fell off the earth and severed all communication. Gram and Gramps vanish into thin air, and my kids pick up on it. I want to shield them from the truth, so when they start asking questions I beat around the bush, evade the issue. They adore their grandparents, and frankly this has nothing to do with them. They don't deserve to be brought into this pandemonium, and I don't want to subject them to any more drama. I hate playing games with two families, but isn't that what a mom is supposed to do – spare her children from unnecessary hurt and disappointment? Besides, enough is enough--I want them out of the life from which I'm trying so desperately to escape.

Still, waiting for my parents to make contact drives me bonkers, and I call them diligently morning, noon, and night to try to make amends. But they're obstinate and won't take my calls. Self doubt begins to rear its ugly head. *Did I make the right decision? Perhaps my words were too harsh, maybe I was totally insensitive to their needs? Who knows! I only know I'm not handling anything too well these days. Bottom line is I feel a great deal of remorse for what I've done, like I'm eating my words now, and they taste like shit...*

What about me? Don't I deserve more? What about my dreams? When will it ever be my time to shine? I'd fume, only to end up thinking *look where this has gone now, Lord--when will this hellish nightmare end? It's my fault--I care too deeply about Mom and Dad —they're my everything! But I have a precious family of my own now that should come first, no matter what. And I have to be free so I can live my life!*

We go about our daily lives over the next few months, saying little about the elephant in the room. Occasionally Mom and Dad show up at family events or the kids' activities, but there is no connection, and everyone feels the strain. We speak only pleasantries because, really, there isn't anything else to say. How odd that they're both still alive, yet something has clearly died. My world has completely shattered before my eyes, yet I know there's no turning back. As I said before, there are no "do over's" in life; our relationship seems irreparable.

Until one day, out of the blue, my phone rings again. It's Mom on the line. Her voice quivers and I can sense her head shaking like it does when she's uptight and anxious. A heartsick feeling overcomes me.

"What is it Mom? What's going on?"

"We just left the doctor's office, and I have bad news. Your father is gravely ill. We were just told he has cancer and the prognosis isn't good."

Speechless, I hang up the phone and stare off into space for what seems like a coon's age. I can't believe what I've just heard. Dad has *cancer*. Holy Toledo! He's had almost every ailment known to man and constantly asks me for doctor referrals. He wishes I'd married a doctor to "fix" him, he'd say. I kid you not—it was a longstanding joke in the family for years. Through every ordeal, operation, procedure--the list is endless--Dad always survived. When the chips were down, he'd pull though and we'd all shake our heads in astonishment. It's like he had nine lives or something. But never has it been a disease as dreaded as the "Big C." I'm petrified for him.

My primal instinct is to dash over to their house and take charge. I know exactly what to do--I'm an oncology nurse for God's sake. This is my field of expertise. In the back of my mind I hear Amy saying "their situation is only going to get worse, are you equipped to handle that?" I prayed this day would never come, but here it is staring me in the face. My old programming starts to kick in and I want to revert to my old familiar ways.

"What should I do, Lord?" I ask out loud. "They need me bad! This is a matter of life or death--how can I ignore them?"

Then I hear a message loud and clear. It's a revelation, a moment of truth:

Relinquish Rita and John to us--it's time.

"I can't!" I protest.

You must! is the response. *You must do this, break the cycle, and free yourself!*

In a moment of clarity, I make one of the most arduous decisions of my life. Monumental, it takes days to arrive, but my heart knows it's the right thing to do. I choose to bow out, call it quits, so that Mom and Dad have this last dance together, just the two of them--the way it should be.

Chapter Twelve
Trusting in a Higher Power

There are no coincidences in life; every event unfolds in divine order. Miracles can and will take place, if you're willing to suspend all doubt and allow grace to flow through you. I'm forty-four years old when my dad decides to "graduate" from this earthly plane.

No great surprise to anyone in our immediate family, as truly he's suffered a great deal. John White endured much mental and emotional pain his entire life and it was time for him to go home. A tremendous amount of fear surrounds this frail man, never able to express his love for another human being. However, that is about to change as his transformation begins.

His stroke--a complication from cancer--leads quickly to paralysis, and subsequently to a comatose state. Talk about losing complete control of your body *and* mind! In the hospital he fights back initially, thrashing about in his bed like a convicted prisoner being brutally persecuted and put to his death. Being tied down worsens the situation, and frankly I find it quite inhumane. It's difficult to watch, but with proper medication and kind, healing hands, he stops resisting and it seems almost as if he's surrendered to a higher power. Indeed, he's chosen this path as the means by which to arrive at his final destination. Everything is in divine order.

Dad loves a party and being surrounded by family--especially his grandchildren. This gathering proves no different and turns into the biggest farewell party of all. When John lapses into a coma, his true, authentic essence emerges. He becomes docile, gentle, and fearless. He allows us to hold his hand, touch his arm, and stroke his hair. The piece of him he'd forgotten--dormant for so long--now springs to life. Fear dissipates, and all that remains is unconditional love.

The realization that there's always a bigger picture unfolding if we just sit back, take a breath, and pause is liberating to me. Patience is indeed a virtue. Compassion fills the space previously occupied by anger and hate. Dad exudes more love from his heart to mine in his dying state than I've ever experienced before. Connected now on a very deep level, I feel empathically his life's afflictions and, in my heightened state of awareness, understand who he really is. With new eyes, I no longer see him as an abusive father, but rather as a wounded soul who never allowed himself to feel. Deep down in his core John is a good, decent man, a child of God. How could he have given to me that which he'd never allowed himself--the gift of love? Yes, there would be more forgiveness work for me to do, but this precious moment in time is the beginning of my healing process.

Family and friends begin to gather at his bedside and reminisce about his life. We share stories, tell jokes about his idiosyncrasies, and laugh and cry simultaneously—exactly as he would have wished. We huddle around him and pray together the evening prior to his passing. At this point, when I see him struggling, a sweet cherub voice rises up from within. A message comes loud and clear: *Pat, lead us now in prayer.* We all circle John's bed and hold hands as I speak the rest of the message as it comes forth:

"Dear Lord, we are here tonight for your son, John," I begin. "We ask that he be comforted as he prepares to return home. Shower him with love and grace, and fill his heart with peace. We know he will be guided into the light by his angels and family members who have already crossed. It is his time and we humbly bless him and set him free. Amen."

I open my eyes and notice that Dad is much calmer. His breathing softer now, the congestion in his chest has subsided and his pulse is less bounding. He can't speak, but telepathically communicates to me his next wish. Again, my higher self instructs me to reach into my pocket and pull out a crystal I'd placed there hours ago but completely forgotten about until now! I hold this precious gem and, dumbfounded, read the inscription. *Love* is the word engraved across it. Instinctively, I place it gently over Dad's heart, and together we simultaneously witness what follows.

Dad's cheeks begin to quiver, and in an instant a bright smile lights up his entire face. Moved to tears, each of us recognizes this testimony to the true power of the divine and the angelic realm! We all understand the magnitude of what love can do--and conquer--without uttering a word. Dad had been unable to move the right side of his face from the stroke, but for a miraculous moment he lets us know all is well. Without a doubt, he's not alone--the room is filled with celestial beings preparing him for his flight.

Not only does my father enjoy a party, often he's the last one to leave. Why should his last hurrah be any different? Clearly he savors this time and isn't ready to depart just yet. He's met with eleven of his twelve grandchildren and is waiting now to see Matthew, his firstborn grandson, who's scurrying to the hospital from out of state.

Dad will have it no other way. Talk about who's still at the helm! We honor his last wishes and wait with him. When Matthew arrives we give them sacred space to meet privately, as they haven't seen each other in quite some time. A beautiful exchange of unconditional love from grandfather to grandchild follows. A sense of peace resonates within the confines of the hospital room and within each one of us--all is well. Loose ends seem to have been tied up--clearly it's up to John to make the next move.

The entire family leaves the hospital the following morning to get some rest and a fresh change of clothes. I can't sleep a wink and return quickly to my father's bedside. Not a soul is around when I enter the room, which I think is quite odd. On the other hand, I'm grateful to be able to spend a few minutes with him alone. I close the door softly behind me and pull up a chair. I know what to do next intuitively, as if an omnipotent presence is guiding me--I have no doubts or questions. All time and space feels suspended, as if we're in another realm where absolutely anything is possible.

I bring my lips to his left ear ever so gently and whisper, "Hi Dad, it's me, Pat." I have a strong urge to touch his lips, so I do. I run my fingers along his newly shaven face and tell him how soft and supple he feels. The smell of his aftershave cologne seeps into my nasal passages and I'm reminded of how much time he used to spend looking in the mirror—hours and hours and hours, primping and fixing his hair. Brushing and flossing his pearly whites. I chuckle for a minute and know he gets it.

I feel his locks of hair and see with my own eyes the beauty of this man--this man who gave me life, who brought me into this world. I lay my head on his chest and feel the beat of his heart as it pulsates through his body. It sends a warm vibration down my spinal column and into the core of my being. I have never connected with him on this level, yet there is a sense of déjà vu. We have indeed been here before. Tears cascade down my face-- warm and salty, they taste good. They are tears of joy. This is a superb memory, one I don't want to ever forget.

"I want you to know how much I love you, Dad. Even though you could never say those words to me, deep down inside, I knew you did. I want to thank you for all you've done for me, because if it weren't for you I would never have gone to nursing school. You pushed me to do it--you knew it's what I was destined to become. I am forever grateful. There is a part of me that wishes you were not leaving, as I'm just getting to know the real you, but I understand you've completed your soul's journey. It's time now. Go in peace, go in joy, and get some much needed rest--you deserve it. Enjoy your next life and be happy. I'll cherish you always and look forward to reuniting with you one day."

I could feel his spiritual arms envelop me and hold me tightly. I didn't want to ever let him go. It was love, pure love. I felt safe, secure, validated, and heard. For the *first time* in my life I connected with my dad. It was the father-daughter understanding for which I'd always longed. No more false pretenses, we knew each other's stories and were good with one another. All was well. I couldn't have orchestrated a more fitting farewell.

I lift my head off his chest and gaze into his hazel eyes. I peer deep down into his soul and see God--in all his magnificence and beauty, I see him. How exquisite! There's nothing more to say, nothing more to do. Our work is done. Our life together, here on this earthly plane, is now finished.

It's said that hearing is one of the last senses to go for the dying. I firmly believe this, as I experienced it firsthand. I believe also that--if you have a heart-to-heart connection with your loved one--no words need be spoken and still the message will be clearly received. Love prevails, even in the midst of your loved one's dying.

My mom and sister Marilyn arrive shortly after and I ask them where they've been. They tell me the nursing staff explained that they'd given my dad the opportunity to choose whether he wanted to be alone or not as death was drawing near. They said that some people prefer to die alone in private, and sometimes they don't want to burden their family, but my dad had absolutely--without question—stated he did not wish to be without his family for his graduation. I know this to be true--I sense it with my whole being!

One by one, we return for the final farewell. A sense of serenity fills the air as his breathing becomes slow and effortless.

We impart our blessings and wish him well on the next part of his journey. As he takes his last breath we witness yet another miracle. He raises his paralyzed arm high in the air as if to wave goodbye, and then ever so gently lowers it down to rest on his abdomen. A glowing white light surrounds him and he looks radiant. Dad has graduated. He's going home...

We return home, and Todd and I retreat to our beautiful meditation garden. Dad spent a significant amount of time here in his final months. Often I'd find him sitting in the Adirondack chair amongst the flowers and birds, resting and reflecting, perhaps contemplating his life and preparing for his next venture.

It seemed fitting to be in the space my father had relished so. We sit in the garden in solitude, simply being and remembering this unique man. Out of the corner of my eye, I witness the glory and richness of life once again. Perched on the branch of the birch tree is my dad's favorite—a hummingbird! Amazed at this rare sight and that this creature is so tranquil and undisturbed, he stays just long enough for us to recognize his presence and then takes off like a helicopter in flight.

Todd and I glance at each other, and instinctively read each other's thoughts. To us it's a clear sign that Dad is in heaven, and that understanding brings us both great comfort. Messages come to us in all kinds of mysterious ways, and if we're open to receiving them, these gifts will manifest before our eyes. I allow the veil to be lifted so I can see the truth of all that is.

The circle of life is complete. I've witnessed a transformation unlike anything I've ever seen—to observe a man who'd been impatient, steamed up, pissed off and irate his entire life change into a benevolent and loving being was almost unimaginable! Clearly I'd been shown the intelligence and power of universal energy--the life force that sustains each of us from one life into the next. If you trust in a higher power, magic and miracles will happen—it's truly that simple.

Chapter Thirteen
Letting Go

Life is queer, with its twists and turns, as every one of us learns at some point. Have you ever held onto someone so tight cuz you just couldn't let them go? You didn't want to lose them because without them in your life, you might cease to exist. I *have...*

Two weeks after my father's death, Mom is admitted to the hospital with congestion in her lungs. Initially, I think perhaps she's simply exhausted, but soon realize that's wishful thinking on my part. Not even close to the truth--just a stupid notion of mine, dreamer that I am.

We all let out a big sigh of relief as she rallies briefly, but it turns out to be very short-lived. Mom's health declines before my eyes, yet I'm in denial. I've just buried my dad and am looking forward to spending some quality time with her one-on-one, mother and daughter, and am not at all prepared for her to leave this world! Not yet!

When a loved one tells you they'll be dying soon, *listen up!* Pay close attention, as this may be the reality of the situation. Our loved ones prepare themselves and their family members for their transition. When Mom tells me she wants to join Dad in heaven, my life catapults into a state of frenzy. I pretend I don't hear her, but she repeats the dreaded words again—emphatically: "I am ready to die..."

I quickly assess her from head to toe, and can tell from my nursing experience that she's alert, oriented, and retains all of her faculties still. On oxygen round the clock, her vital signs and oxygen level are stable, but her hands and head tremble from all the medication she's taken for her lung issues. She can't walk very far without getting winded, but at least she is still alive. That works for me! So when Rita talks about dying, I do everything in my power to change the subject. In emotional turmoil, I can't wrap my head around this one—it's my way of staying in command. Honestly, though, fate is in the driver's seat, not me.

I shut her out when I feel I'm going to lose it. I stop listening —this is way too agonizing! I can't sleep. I can't eat. I think about her day and night, as I see clearly the signs of impending death. The same song plays over and over in my head for days:

"Mom, I don't want you to go!"

"But Pat, I want to go."

"I don't want you to go!"

"But Pat, I need to go."

"I don't want you to go!"

"But Pat, I must go, it's time..."

I pray for guidance and the strength to help me through whatever will come next. Ultimately, it isn't my choice, or my place, to force my wishes on Mom any longer. When I open my eyes to see *her* truth, I understand clearly that Mom is not living—she's merely existing. It's selfish of me to put my needs ahead of hers. Without a doubt, she is plum tuckered out. The most selfless, loving act would be to abide by her wishes and let her go.

Suddenly, something shifts within, and almost immediately support and a whole lot of courage arrive. I move forward with ease and without hesitation--I know what I have to do to tie up loose ends and prepare for what's to come.

I choose to open my heart fully to this woman who gave me life, and to honor her with the dignity she truly deserves. No more bogus pretenses, discord, or chaos, the barriers drop and we celebrate her final days together in harmony, peace, and unconditional love. I reckon that's exactly what heaven is like!

Dr. Ira Byock, a palliative care physician, and the author of a most poignant book called *The Four Things That Matter Most,* points out four simple statements that provide a nurturing, tremendously healing environment for all when a loved one is dying. They are: *Please forgive me; I forgive you; thank you; and I love you--*some of the most profound words ever spoken from one spiritual being to another. These words can alleviate the deepest wounds and bridge the widest gaps for generations to follow. They facilitate the sacred space that allows the dying to pass in blissful peace, while assuring family members that no stone has been left unturned. Let nothing be left unsaid. Not always simple to do, it often takes a leap of faith to cast away all fears and lay your cards —I mean your *heartstrings*--on the table. It's a conscious choice and the opportunity is there for everyone, no matter how broken and damaged the relationship.

I stop fighting my mother's decision, cherish her for who she is, and begin to experience miracles! I pay her a visit in the hospital four days before she dies and, upon entering her room, notice the curtain draped around her bed, so I sneak a peek. Unprepared for what I see, I gasp. Attempting to give herself a sponge bath, Mom is clearly no longer capable of this task. She huffs and puffs, extremely short of breath. The tip of her nose and her earlobes are dark blue, as are her fingertips and toes.

It's extremely difficult to see her in this deteriorated and pathetic condition. I know she's not getting enough oxygen--not a good sign. She can barely speak. I summon her nurse promptly, who rectifies the situation immediately with appropriate drugs to alleviate Mom's restlessness. Within minutes, Mom is calm, and so am I.

I climb into her bed and wrap my arms around her. She snuggles her head into the nape of my neck and drapes her arms around me. We hold each other tightly. I smell the Prell shampoo in her silver white locks of hair, so fresh and clean, like a warm summer's day. I feel her chest rise and fall with each and every breath she takes--every breath another opportunity for life. Be it one more minute or one more hour, I cherish each and every one. My own body becomes warm and flush, and with that the tears began to flow. I don't try to stop them, I don't care one bit who sees me or what they think. Nothing matters anymore, except being with my mom.

I touch her shoulders softly and gently massage her back, encouraging her tense muscles to relax. She moans softly as her body melts into mine. I cup her pale white cheeks with my fingertips and caress them, too. I gaze deeply into her eyes. Neither of us speaks; her dark green eyes say it all. They smile at me with such beauty and radiance that any sadness I feel evaporates into thin air.

I sense her energy, her inner strength, so powerful and alive. Her spirit is vibrant and well. I know she's going to be okay no matter what. This woman, my mother, lying here with me, completely mesmerizes me. I hold her in my arms as she asks my forgiveness. I reciprocate with the same rhetorical question. I comfort her as a mother tends her newborn. I caress her and touch her so she never forgets her perfection and divinity, and always knows how special she is--so she remembers what she forgot eons ago: That she is pure *love*...and then she releases those mystical, magical words ever so divinely:

"Pat, I love you so much. I never, ever stopped loving you, despite our difficulties over the years. I'm *so* proud of you as a daughter, sister, and mother! Thank you for all you've done for me--I will treasure our relationship always. You have a piece of my heart forever."

Tears stream down both our cheeks by this time. I don't know if I can formulate the words I so desperately need my mother to hear. This is the final act, the last call. I need to speak my truth and make peace with her. I choose to forgive and hopefully to be forgiven. This is it! I want--*need*--to get it right.

"Mom, thank you for being the best mom you could be. You're kindhearted, patient, and loving--you helped me raise my three children, and you were always available to lend a hand. Simple and ordinary are your ways. Yet you're an extraordinary woman! I love you, and let you go now to be with Dad! I look forward to our reuniting again, one day..."

I depart the hospital that precious day a different being--a different daughter, a different mother. Not less old, but a whole lot wiser. You may wonder why. I'd say it's because I simply decide to let go and let God; I stop being in charge. And when I do, it feels like the weight of the world lifts from my shoulders. No longer compelled to make any decisions regarding my mother's health, I don't have to fix a thing. Besides, it's *her* life and her free will to decide if and when she is ready to die. The Creator will take over from here and guide her on her way. My work is done and I can step aside, ever so confident she's in the best of hands! Meanwhile, I'd love my mom, Rita Ann White, with every ounce of my being for as long as *she* chooses to remain on this planet.

Three days later I rally the troops for her farewell party. Dear friends and family from near and far come to my mother's bedside to reminisce one last time and say their goodbyes. Tears and laughter, sadness and joy, all reverberate in the air as we all hug, kiss, hold hands, and embrace anywhere and everywhere. Love prevails and permeates every nook and cranny of her hospital room.

My sister Joanne and I stay with Mom two nights before she dies. Initially quite agitated, she finally settles down into a serene sleep. I sit in the chair by her bed listening to her every sound and watching every movement--I don't want to miss a thing. I hold her hand, rub her arm, and touch her for as long as I'm able. I fall into a deep slumber and awaken to her mumbling words. She talks into the wee hours of the morning, not to me, but most definitely to someone. *Wow,* I think, *she must be having some colossal dream!*

Mom awakens the next morning with the sweetest smile on her face, and my sister and I swear she looks younger! She tells us that she met her deceased mother-in-law the night before, and that they'd made amends. Absolution had taken place and all is well. She's so delighted to go home and be with her family in heaven. Mom glows and I can palpate this sensation within my own body. The angelic realm is preparing for her flight and it's almost departure time.

I have the privilege of staying with Mom her last evening in her physical body. Honestly, she really isn't much company, that's for sure, but it makes no difference to me. I just want to be with her! She snores loudly for most of the evening, but at one a.m. she becomes edgy, distressed, and hollers out for help. The night nurse checks her vital signs then increases her medication to calm her and help her breathing become less labored. I am in total agreement with her care as Mom is now in the process of actively dying and I promised her she'd be kept comfortable...and I am going to make damn sure I keep my word.

"Is there anything else you need, Rita?" the nurse inquires.

"I'm *afraid,*" is Mom's response. The nurse gives me a nod, as if to say, "You've got this one, Pat," then exits the room to give us our space.

I pull down the side rail to Mom's bed and lean over so she can see me. She looks like a child just awakened from a terrifying nightmare. I take her hand in mine and squeeze it tight to let her know I'm right there by her side. I'm well aware she is heavily medicated, but clearly something is spooking her.

"What are you afraid of, Mom?" I ask her gently.

"I don't know," is her reply.

I sit on the edge of her bed and rub my fingers gently across her forehead for quite some time. I smile warmly down at her and tell her she's safe--just like she used to tell me when I woke up screaming from a bad dream as a child.

"I won't leave you, Mom--you're not alone and won't be during this process," I reassure her. "Scouts honor! Our family will be right by your side, just like we were for Dad. Whenever you feel ready to leave your body...it's all right to do so."

This seems to appease her, thank goodness. I kiss her on the forehead, tell her "I love you, Mom," but she doesn't reply. It doesn't matter anyway, because I feel her love everywhere. Her presence, her spirit, is so strong it's as if she's already soaring. She basks in her own radiance.

"Sweet dreams, Mom," I smile down at her. "You are so beautiful to me."

Finally, she drifts off into a deep sleep and by seven a.m. Mom is no longer responsive. In a coma now, her time is drawing near. By the end of the day, our family is gathered together once again to bid Rita White farewell. Through tears, sadness, laughter, gratitude, and much love, we say our goodbyes. Hers is a perfect graduation, just like Dad's, with absolutely no fear involved, simple and unassuming—just like my mom, just as she'd lived her life. No struggle or suffering in her departure, she lets go with grace and dignity. So many lessons, I am learning!

I'm honored to be present during this rite of passage, and to share these rich, splendid, unforgettable moments--moments that we, as human beings, can't possibly create on our own, as they are manifested by a much deeper wisdom, the wisdom of the universe. The circle of life is complete once again--merely the continuation of the miracles begun with my father's passing. I find great solace in knowing they are together once again, for all eternity...

Chapter Fourteen
The Darkness

I miss Mom terribly. I miss seeing her face and hearing her voice. Visiting my parents' apartment proves challenging. Dad's deerskin moccasins sit by the front door as usual and Mom's beige Cherry and Webb pocketbook is perched upright on the kitchen table. Everything is as it should be, yet nothing is the same—it's all changed drastically. No one greets me as I walk into the kitchen, and that's the oddest feeling in the world. I pinch myself to see if I'm hallucinating. I'm not.

This is my new reality. My whole world turned upside down, I'm reeling still from it. I walk slowly from room to room as tears cascade down my cheeks. I glance up at our family wedding pictures on the wall and am overtaken by sobs. Good times, bad times, whatever kinds of times, they're all history now...

Overwhelmed, I realize my parents are gone--forever. *I must move on, keep a stiff upper lip—it's all for the best.* I wipe away my remaining tears, plant that hideous, fake smile on my face, and shut the apartment door for the last time. This part of my life is over and it's time to close the book on that chapter...

For days on end I call my parents house phone repeatedly.

Mom's voice, still on the answering machine, makes me feel--for a brief second--like she's still alive, like I could reach through that phone line and grab a hug or just chat with her for a wee bit. I hang up and call again and again until my body shakes with such intense grief that I have to stop. This is mental torture and I'm clearly at a breaking point--ready for the booby hatch if I don't get some control over my life, that's a given!

In all honesty I am completely overwhelmed physically, emotionally, and mentally after Mom's death. Yes, I understand the ramifications of all that's taken place over the past short few months, and I'm truly at peace with the outcome, but at times the sadness is unbearable as I attempt to find some semblance of calm in my own life once again. *I try.* I really do, but I can't shake it.

Eight months later, still despondent, I go through the motions as if I'm moving forward with my life, but it's only an act. Inside I'm still singing the blues. I manage to keep my funky feelings tucked inside my heart—don't want to bother anyone. They might think I'm cracking up. *Aren't I supposed to be able to handle this on my own? Why can't I? What's wrong with me?* I thought I *was* losing it...my mind-body is still stuck in the muck, and I just can't get out. A quadrant of my heart feels ripped out, and I actually experience physical pain in the mid-thorax area. This sensation of intense tightness brings me to my knees, and let me tell you, it's downright scary!

"Am I having a heart attack?" I scream. *It sure feels like it! Please, please go away--I have no time for this now. Let me be so I can heal!* This pain is clearly nothing to mess with, and I recognize that. I've had plenty of nursing experience with cardiac patients and know that if it doesn't go away within five to ten minutes, I'll have to seek medical attention.

I begin to count backward from one hundred to one. I concentrate diligently on each and every number and at around twenty-two a weird thing happens--the pain subsides. Don't know why, only know I'm not about to question it. *Wow, I guess that was a crash course in stress management, Pat! You need to slow down and take better care of yourself. You've just had a huge warning!*

My heavy heart and I sink lower and lower into the abyss of despair. How much lower can I go before I'm completely swallowed up and devoured? I'm beginning to understand the effect stress can have on one's body. I've certainly been under major strain for quite some time. *Don't have to tell me again--I hear you loud and clear!* my brain shouts. *But do I?*

Suddenly, and without my permission, life jerks me forward into the next phase of my journey. When you think things can't get any worse, hang on a minute! I find out the arduous way, of course--seems the school of hard knocks is my favored route.

Chapter Fifteen
Falling Apart

I awaken from my breast biopsy groggy and sore, my left breast bandaged and the small pea-sized lump now gone.

"The preliminary pathology report will probably be ready tomorrow," my surgeon says. Frankly, I'm quite optimistic, since the growth is so small, but I don't hear from him the following day and my optimism begins to fade. Good news travels quickly, bad news does not, at least in my case...

Two days after my biopsy and several phone calls later, I receive my results:

"You have breast cancer," I hear my doctor say.

Did he just say what I think he did? Am I crazy? He must have made a mistake! Maybe I didn't hear him correctly! I can't have cancer! Not me! I'm an oncology nurse--I take care of people who have cancer. I'm not supposed to get it! Something's very wrong, this can't be possible! Wake me from this nightmare someone--please!

*Cancer, cancer, cancer...*the word penetrates my psyche. Drastic words no human wants to hear in her lifetime—*ever!* After all, once was plenty with Dad. I begin to entertain all kinds of hair-raising thoughts.

"Pat, are you still there?" I hear my surgeon ask. "Do you have any questions?"

I want to answer him, but I can't. Nothing comes out. Not a sound. I feel numb. I want to flee, escape this ghastly daydream, but my body won't move. It remains heavy and lifeless, as if paralyzed from head to toe.

Dr. P. finishes his dictation--I don't remember saying goodbye, nor do I recollect hanging up the phone. I haven't a clue what he just said to me! It's a big blur, and all I can remember hearing is the freaking word *cancer...how I abhor that god damned word!*

Minutes pass before I look down at the telephone lying on my desk. I pick it up gingerly and whisper what I didn't have the guts to ask just moments before: "Doc, am I gonna *die?*"

Alone and empty inside, it's as if every ounce of energy's been zapped from my body. In a heartbeat, the life force in me departs and something within dies. Impossible for me to put into words, I think: *I can't even wrap my head around this one, so how can I explain it? I don't understand any of it! It's just a feeling--a knowing deep within my core.* Life throws me a curve ball and I don't have the foggiest idea how to hit. *Jesus Christ, what am I supposed to do now?*

Random thoughts ricochet through my brain like firecrackers

lighting up the night. *Should I call Todd and Patrick, summon them home to give them the bad news? Do I share this information immediately with Colleen and Erin, waiting anxiously in the next room? Do I scream out loud? This sucks, God, and it can't be happening to me!*

My childhood was pure hell, now you throw me this bull crap on top of everything else? How dare you torture my family! What did they do to deserve this? I despise you and all of your righteousness! Damn all of it, damn you!

I've finally found salvation with Todd, Colleen, Erin, and Patrick. Do you know how long and hard I've worked to get to this place in my life—to finally have created the family for which I've always longed? It's been barely a year since Mom and Dad died, and I had high hopes we'd be heading into a new phase of life by now--a more serene, gentle way of being. But no, you allow life to sucker-punch me again! What is this bullshit? Bad karma that destroys everyone I care about? Haven't I suffered enough loss? Haven't I paid my fuckin' dues?

Help me, help me, somebody guide me! I feel so lost, and I'm scared stiff! I've just been told I have cancer, and I don't know how to handle this one! I feel like my life is spinning out of control--I'm out of control! Someone please take over--I want my mommy!

Half dazed, I somehow manage to collect myself and make my

way into the living room to give my daughters the verdict. My heart sinks as I look into their eyes and tell them I have cancer. By the looks on their faces they already knew. I feel their tension escalate, and I desperately want to take away their heartache - *still trying to shelter them from life's trials!* - but I cannot.

Breaking the news to Todd is harder still. The forlorn look in his baby blues kills me. Not a word is spoken; we embrace like we have never embraced before. This hug is vastly different. He holds me for the longest time. It's not casual, it's not playful--nope it's real serious. It's an *I'm petrified, don't leave me!* kind of hug. Our bodies begin to shake as we attempt to console one another, to hold each other up. Sobs take precedence as our emotions overcome us. We let it out, let it out, let it out, until we both finally run out of tears--for the time being.

Todd takes my cheeks into his big, burly hands and says, "Pat, we'll get through this together, as a family." I want so to trust and believe his every word. But deep down I know that he cannot fix this dilemma, nor can he protect me from my fate. It all hurts so badly right now, it really does. I've never in my life seen Todd look so alarmed. I have to stay composed.

From that moment forward I try to keep it together. *I have to be strong,* I tell myself, *have to be in charge!* But my inner child whispers *fall apart!*

Chapter Sixteen
Wake Up Sweet Child, It's Time

I've been asleep for a very long time. Needed a sledge hammer cracked over my skull to get my attention and awaken me from my slumber. God was whispering in my deaf ear for years, but I neglected her advice. So one day God roars, and I bounce out of bed, land flat on my ass, gaze up at her, and say: "Ok, I'm listening *now!*"

Suddenly I become angry. In fact, my diagnosis--this cancer-- fills me with rage! For a brief moment it paralyzes me, too—that's the worst. But my rage wins out, as it causes me to rise to action, and I find myself attempting to take the reins back even though my mind reels with anxiety. I begin to prepare myself for what's to come, and realize the importance of getting my cancer treatment team in place *asap!* This becomes a crucial priority, as it takes my mind off the negative, perpetual hamster wheel on which it's begun to run and helps me feel I'm doing something positive for myself.

Hours after receiving my diagnosis I schedule a meeting with one of the oncologists with whom I work, and believe me I'm so grateful to be seen pronto! I bring Todd, Colleen, and a large notebook with me to the appointment. I figure the more ears the better--they can listen and record vital information if I start to space out. They can speak up for me if I don't feel strong enough to do so. I seem right now to weave in and out of several different realities. It's the oddest sensation to walk through the sturdy oak doors of the clinic knowing that I'm the patient this time and *not* the nurse. *I detest this--it feels so bizarre. It's terrifying and I don't like it! I'd give my eye tooth right now to be on the other side of the fence, so to speak...*

My legs feel like Jell-O as I make my way into the cold, sterile exam room. *Someone please pinch me and tell me this isn't happening! Wake me up from this nightmare and let me go back to six months ago when my life was normal, before I discovered this damn lump in my breast! Please just let me get through this appointment and then you (my pysche) can act up all you want!*

Although I think I've made an agreement with myself, suddenly a voice in the cobwebs of my mind pipes up: *Yeah, sure, we won't act up right now, but we'll be back, don't you fret... Frig, my mind is playing tricks on me again!* I remind myself sarcastically that my life has never been normal. Yo*u know that, Pat, and no, you can't go back!*

We wait for Dr. S. to arrive with my verdict, and it's so quiet we can hear a pin drop. Life or death...guilty or not guilty, it feels like I am awaiting sentencing. In an odd way I reckon I am... he's the expert you know, doling out recommendations for treatment; feels like my life is in his hands, sort of. Immediately upon entering the room, Dr. S. puts me at ease.

"How are you doing Pat?" he asks.

I really want to tell him I'm panic-stricken, enraged, desolate, and close to jumping off the nearest bridge—in layman's terms, I'm going cuckoo! Instead, filled with an intense sense of sadness as I gaze at Todd and Colleen, I tell Dr. S. I'm okay. A ginormous fib! I don't want to scare everyone away with my *feelings*. Such a big lie, I can almost feel my nose growing longer by the second!

Dr. S. peruses my records and proposes a tentative treatment plan. Right now my case is pretty cut-and-dried: I have stage 1B breast cancer for which the standard treatment is radiation followed by hormone therapy. I understand I must still undergo further testing to determine if the cancer has metastasized or spread to other vital organs, which would then alter the current plan. Dr. S. is optimistic and, even though I'm only forty-five years-old and have breast cancer, he tells me I am quite healthy. Kind of an oxymoron, wouldn't ya say? But I understand what he means: I have no other serious illnesses with which to contend. I breathe a sigh of relief—for now...

I have tons of questions and he allows me all the time I need.

There's no hurry, no rush, and I unwind a wee bit. I permit Todd and Colleen to stay in the room while I'm examined, and feel safe with them present. Dr. S. is gentle as he softly presses around my battle scar--the first of many.

"So far, so good," he says. "You're healing nicely. Do you have any other questions, Pat?"

I do not. I leave the appointment much calmer than when I arrived because we--my team and I--are moving forward with a plan to help me get well! I am one hundred percent confident about Dr. S., as he is brilliant, compassionate, and possesses an excellent bedside manner. A no-brainer for me, I must have the complete package--I'll settle for nothing less. Hey, it's my life at stake here...

I require a second surgical procedure two weeks later to remove remaining cancer cells still present at the original tumor site, and while I look like the same old Pat on the outside-- confident, cool, got it together kind of girl--inside I'm falling apart at the seams. Cancer brings out my worst fears imaginable and makes me feel vulnerable, weak, and alone. I fall immediately into victim mode, as some cancer patients do. Neither right nor wrong, good nor bad, it just is.

I lay in my hospital bed attempting to calm my mind and body despite my internal uneasiness, which seems to get the better of me for the billionth time. I'm sick to my stomach, undeniably in pain, and my left breast feels tattered and torn. The second surgery on this breast is now complete but further testing for the inexplicable pain in my abdomen is necessary. Weary from being poked, probed, and prodded up the yin-yang, I am a monstrosity. I want to go home, but can't until my gut can hold down some food. I've got a long way to go--my gastrointestinal tract is currently closed for repairs! At least, that's what it's telling me...

I close my eyes for a brief moment, and hear the pitter-patter of feet enter the room. *Who is it now?* I wonder. *Go away!* I open my eyes begrudgingly to see Colleen standing before me. Drawn, exhausted, and anxious, she seems an uncanny reflection of me. Without hesitation she pulls up a chair beside my bed and sits down. I am too weak for chatter. She gets that, so we sit in the quiet. I hate that she sees me this way--discombobulated and out of sorts. It's certainly not how a girl her age should see her mother. *This is so unfair...*

Without uttering a word, Colleen nonchalantly moves closer to me and ever so gently places her head on my weakened abdomen. Overwhelmed with emotion, I am taken back briefly to when she was a toddler and I'd run my fingers through her beautiful brown Shirley Temple curls. Such precious times! I try hard to fight the tears but they come anyway.

"Mom, I just want you to get better," she whispers softly to me. "I want you to feel well again. I've decided to take a semester off from college so that I can stay home and take care of you."

I gasp at her words, which bite my insides—*hard*. Did she just say "take care of you?" *Good God, have I created another codependent relationship?* My heart fills with agony and breaks at this thought. *Is this what I've passed on to my children? Is this what I've taught her--to become a caretaker? Shame on me! What a terrible role model I've been if this is what she thinks she must be.* I cannot--*will not!*--allow her to lose her identity or her sense of self because of me.

"Off to school you must go, Colleen. I will be a-okay." She's not buying it--she knows me too well and doesn't want to upset the applecart anymore than it's already been upset. She leaves as I request, so I can be alone with myself, my phobias and insecurities.

Frankly God, I ain't got a clue what the future holds for me; I don't know how this story is going to turn out--and to be honest, I'm as spooked as they are! I have no idea how to handle all these feelings, and it makes me loco!

Will I be present to witness my three sweet children get married? Am I going to be alive long enough to hold that first precious grandchild in my arms? Will I have the opportunity to grow old with my husband-- my true love--and live out our dreams together as we'd planned? Or am I going to suffer in misery and torment and live only a few more months? *I don't know what to do anymore, God, I don't know what to say!*

So for the most part, I say nothing. It's been two weeks since my life went haywire. I should say *our* life, since this cancer diagnosis affects my husband and three children as deeply as it does me. I see the frightened look in their eyes. I feel it in the way we embrace, as if it might be for the last time. I sense their suffering and it's killing me!

Chapter Seventeen
Crash Course

The pathology report comes back clean, which is fantastic news--no chemo or mastectomy necessary for Pat! This turns out to be my lucky day! Radiation will be my next step.

I find Dr. A., my radiation specialist, through word of mouth. He comes highly recommended and his office is local. This saves me from having to run into the city every day for five minutes of high dose radiation to eradicate this nasty cancer from my body-- a huge plus!

We start off on the right foot, but our relationship hits a major bump along the way when my "girls" decide to pop out a few more lumps while I'm undergoing radiation. Just for shits and giggles, I guess. But I'm not laughing. Talk about freakin' me out! I didn't think this was part of my treatment plan. The lumps appear on my cancerous left breast and feel just like my original tumor. Flipped out and frantic to speak to Dr. A., I have to meet with his partner instead, since he's off duty. His partner doesn't know my case well enough and recommends I wait two more painstakingly long days for a Dr. A. to return.

Waiting for results when you have cancer is like a death

sentence. My every thought is consumed with the "C" word and how it's already spread to other parts of my body. I'm sure you're thinking that such tainted thoughts lead me to practically put the nails in my coffin. I plead the fifth. You know me too well! Like the hamster on the wheel, I can't seem to run fast enough to get away from my stinkin' thinkin'.

Over-the-top exhausted and overwhelmed with concern, I don't feel like eating or drinking but my body needs adequate nutrition right now. Believe me I'm fully aware of that. That's part of the problem--I know too much. *Kinda wish I wasn't a nurse right now.* The internet isn't helping either—it's got way more information than I need to know and I'm not sure how reliable it is. I really need to shut it down, the computer that is, so hopefully my mind can take a break. Fat chance, Pat's brain is on overdrive and doing everything it can to bring her to her knees to beg for mercy!

Two arduous days later at radiation, I'm kicked in the gut not once but twice. Double the fun, I suppose! First of all, I share with the radiation technologist that I have discovered two new lumps in my left breast. It takes a ton of guts for me to tell her this, you know, cuz I feel real fragile right now. But I do...I open up to her woman to woman--and she lets me down big time. You wanna hear her response to my dilemma?

"What's the big deal? You're getting radiation to that breast anyway," is her *asshole* reply! I can't believe she has the balls to say that to me. Has she got a shred of common sense in that brain of hers? Is she that dumb? How utterly unprofessional!

I feel myself getting all choked up in the throat and I jam my eyes shut so she doesn't see the teardrops beginning to form. I tense up, tightening every muscle in my body. I don't wanna be here right now...I wanna run far away, like I fantasized about when I was a little girl. I trusted her and she kicked me to the curb! *Why do I confide in people? I'm forever disappointed when I open up to people, and it only proves once again that it's easier to bottle shit up, tighten the cork, and keep all of my feelings inside...*

I compose myself, and attempt to get at least partly back together before my visit with Dr. A. Optimistic that he will have a solution to my overactive breast, I'm once again gravely disillusioned.

"Pat, it says here in your chart that you called repeatedly with your concerns about the lumps and were finally seen by my partner two days ago. He states that you were quite anxious--over the top."

"You could say that," I respond. I expect him to empathize with me, to say "I totally understand what you're going through," but instead he chastises me.

"I think you're overreacting," is what comes out of his mouth next. "This isn't really worrisome. We can do an ultrasound, which will most likely show cysts. These usually disappear by themselves. You need to calm down with all of this."

I almost fall off my chair! I can't even begin to fathom what he just said to me. This is total madness! Somebody get me out of this nut ward! Totally fried at this point, my brain has difficulty telling my mouth to formulate even a single word. So there I sit like a dummy, and make no response. Toxic shame swells out of my skin. There's got to be something gravely wrong with me--I must be defective! Everyone treats me like *crap* and I take it! It bites me to the core, and makes me feel inadequate and small, like I'm a *nobody!* I abhor conflict.

It's like I'm an alien in a creature feature movie. Do I speak a different language? Doesn't anyone *get me?* Doesn't anyone in this joint have a caring spirit? Has the world gone completely mad and lost its sense of benevolence? Why didn't I tell him to back off, pound sand, take a hike, and never come back? Why do I simply sit here and not defend myself?

I wander out of the office in a daze, feeling beaten to a pulp. Don't remember getting in my car or driving home, and can't recollect opening the garage door or entering the house. I am in a fog, another world, far, far away from here. But I do remember one thing--crawling into bed and calling Dr. A. every God-awful name in the book that hideous afternoon. My words aren't pretty and they aren't nice and I don't care if he rots in hell one day. I wish only that I'd had the guts to say all of this profanity to his face. But I don't have it in me. For sure, not a mean-spirited person, like the cowardly lion in the *Wizard of Oz*, I can't summon the courage to do what I need to do: *Speak up for myself!*

So I stew over this latest incident for a full week, and after the madness and dust settle, something becomes crystal clear. As if a switch has been flipped, I realize the time has come for Pat to become proactive, and to stand up for herself! She's the only one who can do this—*no one else!* Although not hit by a jolt of lightning, it feels kind of like an epiphany and that gets my brain buzzing. *Instead of reacting to others so defensively all the time, how can I turn it around and become my own best advocate? How can I go from victim to victor?*

I write down exactly what I want to say to Dr. A. and recite it over and over and over again in my head. I do it so many times eventually it is committed to memory. However, I forget every word of my speech--I go blank!--when he saunters into the exam room for a follow up visit. Jittery inside, my palms sweat and my heart pounds erratically, but I can no longer contain myself, and something bursts forth from deep within. I'm about to let loose big time! When Dr. A. asks how I'm doing, the rest becomes history.

"Dr. A, I did not like the way you spoke to me last week." My recitation is brief and to the point. "I'm upset, and rightfully so--I felt you didn't understand what I was going through. Your words were harsh and condescending, and I didn't appreciate them! And it's not okay for you speak to me that way!"

There, I said it! Holy crap, where did this boldness come from? Hell if I know, and it isn't only the doctor who is shocked. Pat--always so meek, mild, and well mannered, normally a pussy cat--came out of her shell! Was I uncomfortable? Heck yeah, but I did it! I had to! How could either of us expect *me* to still be the same old me? *Somebody* had to stand up for *me*—and all the women intimidated and made vulnerable by those in authority; for all the women who might follow in similar footsteps one day. Suddenly intensely alive, I sit up even straighter in my seat after that speech!

Dr. A. did indeed apologize for his harsh words, and that day our relationship changes for the better. My goal was not to criticize him, but to help him see that his words are powerful—they can help or harm an individual in crisis. Underlying his medical knowledge of cancer treatment should be the understanding that dignity, compassion, and hope are sometimes all a patient needs. Broad shoulders and attentive ears are often the best medicine of all.

Did I switch to another doctor? *No!* There was no need, especially since we were now on the same playing field, and I stated clearly my boundaries. He knows now that if he crosses them again I'll be out the door seeking a new physician--no ifs, ands, or buts about it! We develop a new respect for one another that day and I genuinely believe he's becoming a kinder human being.

In turn, he's given me a crash course in assertiveness. I grew a ton that week! Not in stature, of course, but in learning how to find my voice and speak my truth. I require much more training, but at least this is a start. All I know is that this day I mattered--I became a *somebody,* with a voice that deserves to be heard! What a courageous moment in my life!

Chapter Eighteen
Demons, Devils, & Emotional Turmoil

Soon I begin to ask all of the *why* questions: *Why me? Why now?* I consider myself--at the tender age of forty-five--quite healthy, and don't think I fit the criteria of most women my age diagnosed with breast cancer. I'm really quite perplexed...fear lurks in every corner and I can't escape the hold its tenacious claws have on me. Fear accompanies me when I wake up in the morning, follows me throughout the day, and escorts me into the bedroom at night. Demons dance in my head in the silence of darkness, sending evil messages from the neurons of my brain to every cell in my body. They control me totally, as if I'm possessed or brainwashed! I believe everything they say—completely! It is pure evil...I think if I stay active I'll make the demons disappear, but that's merely a temporary mental detour.

Simple daily questions begin to haunt me, and bring much stress and anxiety into my life. I become mentally and emotionally exhausted, like whenever I've tried to put together a puzzle with several missing pieces in the past. Without them I can never succeed in completing it. *What could I have done differently to prevent this?* I wonder. *What did I do to cause it? Did I create this?* These questions go round and round in my brain.

My body decides to join in the fun and becomes a willing participant. If the mind is a victim, the body might as well hitch a ride. So it does just that and my physical symptoms arrive. I develop excruciating pain in various parts of my body--sharp shooting pains that take my breath away and lead me to my new home on the living room floor where I lay curled in the fetal position for relief. Nausea, lack of appetite, and weight loss accompany intermittent low grade fevers, sweats, and palpitations. A myriad of tests all prove negative but the symptoms refuse to abate.

Various doctors do their best to ease my physical symptoms, and I swallow pills that dull the pain temporarily but leave my head foggy and my body fatigued. Pills for nausea, anxiety, depression, insomnia, and loss of appetite that, in turn, create new symptoms. My colon, always a weak area of my body, does a number on me--understandably so, given the preparations and dyes sent surging through my veins and body to determine the stage of my cancer. Clearly though, there's more going on here.

A vicious cycle with no end in sight, my clothes become baggy--I have no spare junk in my trunk. No longer able to hide my intense emotional, mental, and physical pain, I can't deceive anyone anymore, especially myself. My body screams "help!" and I have no choice but to begin to listen. If not, my biggest concern seems inevitable: *I might die!*

Every day feels the same. Life is monotonous and humdrum, yet there's an element of trepidation with each passing hour. Impatient, I want this ordeal behind me—let's fix it, and move on! Somehow, though, deep down inside I know that ain't happening. The bottom line: I can't stay on top of it all and fall instead into a quagmire of deep despair. *Maybe I don't deserve to live anymore!* Ultimately, when I dig deep into the heart of the matter, it really rocks my world. *Am I going to survive this demon called cancer and, if so, for how long?*

My life seems similar to that of a castaway on a desert island, yet this declaration is both incorrect and ludicrous. I'm surrounded by family and friends who want me to lean on them, but I don't even begin to know how to do that. Lean on someone? Accept help? I've been codependent far too long and know only how to give, give, give...receiving doesn't come naturally--if at all!

So I do what I do best. Shut people out. Don't let them in. No, I don't demand to be left alone—march up to my bedroom, slam the door, put up a "keep out" sign, or throw myself a pity party. No, I'm way more subtle than that.

I keep it simple. Don't answer the phone or return calls. Don't respond to knocks on the door. Stay to myself, I guess you could say, and isolate *me* from the rest of the world. *How's that working for you?* you're probably asking. Plain and simple, it isn't...it's eerie being alone, I hate it, but it's what I believe I have to do. Shield the family from the harrowing reality that Mom has cancer. Tell white lies now and again to get by--that's how I convince Erin to go off to college.

"I'm gonna be fine, honey," I tell her, fingers double-crossed behind my back. "Go along now and have fun." Don't know if she falls for it, but she obliges, and frankly, that's one less concern. I despise being dishonest, but what can ya do?

Patrick is another story. Apprehensive about his behavior--he appears distant and aloof much of the time--I persuade myself it's because he's only seventeen. Friends, sports, and girls are on his mind, I reason. I ask Todd to keep an eye on him, keep him in check, but I should know better. The men in my family typically squelch their emotions, too--they simply don't deal with them. I feel awful that I'm unavailable--so much self-condemnation, so much remorse...

Todd looks inconsolable and pitiful, like he's just lost his best friend. Heck--he has! But he acts as if nothing's changed and everything is status quo. Of course, that's an absurdity! Life is anything but normal these days! Conversation between us is minimal and it appears he is shutting down. His spark and charisma have taken a hike, and it tortures me so to see him this fragile. *It's my fault!* I think. *I refuse to torment him with my woes...it's too much to handle right now. How much grief have I caused this man? How much more can he take, God? Why is life so terribly hard?*

Part of me is aching to say "I need you now more than ever, Todd! I feel vulnerable, alone, and frightened--so very frightened! Can you hold me? I feel safe in your arms--it makes this nightmare go away for a while." But I *can't* tell him. You know the saying "honesty is the best policy?" Well, it doesn't apply in my case.

I can't tell Todd and the kids the truth; it would be too much for them to handle. Everyone has their own lives to lead, anyway. I feel like such a burden, a load too cumbersome, and I don't want to drag them down with me. One of us struggling is enough...

So we withdraw from each other on an emotional level as our fear of the unknown overwhelms us. We play a game of pretend, and act like everything is okay. Silly, I know, but it's all we're capable of as we attempt to stay afloat and survive one second at a time. And then I pretend some more and fake it, always trying to dupe someone...

Am I distraught? Heck yeah, but the martyr in me takes

charge and attempts to carry the weight of the world on her shoulders once again. You could have written "stupid" across my forehead. Was I ever gonna get it? Was I ever gonna learn I can't save and protect my family--or the world for that matter—when I can barely save myself?

Chapter Nineteen
The Monkey Mind

*One sheep, two sheep, two million and two sheep...*on and on my thoughts go. Hour after hour after hour. Night after night after night. Not a great sleeper to begin with--oh yeah, already told you that!--I go to bed exhausted and wake up even more fatigued. How is that even possible? Sleeping pills don't do the trick--they merely induce a temporary state of lack of consciousness that relieves me from my incessant thoughts about the fact that I have cancer.

Turning off an active mind proves to be one of the most challenging feats of my cancer journey. How does one halt the negative thoughts that create mental, physical, and emotional turbulence--thoughts that trigger emotions that lead to more anxiety and stress? Truth is, once I wake up, which seems like every bloody hour, my mind dredges up more wretched details about my health. And, hard as I try, and I really do try, I just can't shut off my cerebellum. I can't catch the little critters running rampant through the forest of my brain.

My mind is cluttered and there's no room for additional input. Basically on overload, my brain and I are burning out fast. Both breasts ache. Perhaps one has sympathy pains for the other. Who the heck knows? I'm pooped beyond belief. I wake up tired, go to bed tired, can't work, cook, clean, or do any of the activities I once loved. Frustrated, bitter, and sometimes filled with malice at all that's happened to me, I dwell on the losses I've had to endure.

I feel melancholy, like a part of me expired, just like when Mom, Dad, and my dog Chris were taken away. It tears me up, cuts me to my root, and I feel totally destitute, like I'm all alone in this crazy world...like I'm living in hell here on earth.

I jump out of bed, race into the bathroom, and throw freezing cold water on my face. My heart pounds and beads of perspiration drip off my forehead. I look into the mirror and notice the dark circles that spread like wildfire under both eyes. I resemble an eighty year-old woman, and--God as my witness--I feel like one, too...

Get back to bed, Pat! I snap to myself impatiently. *Go to sleep, you moron!*

Don't you think I want to? I argue with myself. *You think this is fun for me? You think this is a piece of cake? Well, let me tell you a thing or two: This sucks worse than having the measles and chicken pox put together! This stinks a hundred times more than getting my ass whooped when I was a kid!*

I loathe the word cancer and everything it represents. I hate what it's done to my body. I hate that it's tearing my family apart. I hate, hate—hate!--everything about the "C" word. It's taken over my mind and my ability to cope with my new world. I want to go back to my old life! I implore the powers that be. *I'd give anything to be the old me! Can I please go back, please, please--I beg of you!"*

A defiant "*no!*" resounds through my body. I collapse onto the hard tile floor, trembling all over. Metaphorically speaking, I've frequented many mental prisons, but never one as icy cold as this. The feeling is unbearable! It's as if that devil has gripped my brain with his claws, and presses against my skull, harder and harder and harder! *It's too tight! Oh God, stop it—stop! The pain is too much. It's killing me!* Wrapped in a tight ball, I grab onto the base of the toilet and writhe in reaction to my mental discord.

My entire body hurts, especially the pain on my right side, which feels like someone's stabbed me in the back and severed countless nerves and muscles along the way before the knife emerged out of the front of my chest. Sharp and cutting one minute, dull and nagging the next, at times I gasp for air. The situation escalates, sending me into a tailspin, whereupon my stomach fires up and I fear I'm gonna projectile vomit everywhere. Nasty tasting bile rises up in my esophagus. *Stay down, stay down,* I plead, *don't come up, please...*

Should I take a pain pill? Wait--maybe I need something to calm my nerves! Should I swallow some anti-nausea medicine? What should I do? Why can't I figure out what's causing this excruciating pain? It's not normal, I'm sure...the "M" word begins to weave its way into my vocabulary. "M" stands for "metastasis," a dreaded word in the world of cancer, believe me....*what if the cancer has already spread to my liver and bones? Holy crap, that can't be! No, no, no...not me! I can't bear to hear anymore awful news!*

At this point I've had every conceivable test possible. X-rays, cat scans, MRI's, blood work, you name it. They've inserted tubes down my throat and up my rectum. I've been jabbed and stuck a zillion times. The results are amazingly consistent: Negative! I'm given *no* diagnosis for my symptoms. "Great news" is all I keep hearing. "Up yours!" I want to respond.

Some days, God, I think life is just too much to bear and maybe I don't belong here anymore. I've been teetering on the edge of despair for so long, perhaps it's time to call it quits. It's in your hands, God! One thing's for sure--I can't continue to live this way! Besides, this ain't living anyway, it's existing--barely. I tell myself that something has to change, but what? The even bigger question is how?

I look into the bathroom mirror yet again and can no longer deny what's in front of me. I see a pale gaunt face--melancholy, drawn, and fatigued--staring back at me blankly. I see an emaciated body, dwindled to mere skin and bones, at a current all-time low of ninety-eight pounds. I feel vacant, as if the essence of who I am was sucked out of me, and all that's left is an empty hole. I am beginning to look like a corpse.

Who am I? I wonder. I don't know anymore. The even better question is: *Did I ever know?* A teardrop trickles gently down my cheek and a faint voice from the deepest burrow of my soul pleads: *I am in here! Help me!* I wonder: *Should I let go? Can I let go? What will happen if I do?* I am filled with terror.

Where is my faith, that connection to something bigger and greater than myself--the connection that embraced and sustained me through the five-week span of my parents' deaths? Where has it gone? Seems like it's vanished into thin air! Looks like I'm being tested again—yeah, God, I get that! Now what? Maybe there's no more goodness left. Maybe it all got used up with Mom and Dad. Perhaps I'm plum out of luck. You say, trust me, offer it up, believe in me, take my hand! What if I do, and it's not there—your hand, I mean...then what? Do you have an answer for me, God? Enlighten me, would ya.. why the hell should I put my faith in you?

One thing I know for sure: I can't resist any longer! I can't hold on one more second! I'm completely out of sync with my spiritual truth, and clearly my life is not working on any level. How can I reclaim a life filled with purpose and value? Who can I trust with my life? Who will guide me? Can I really begin anew? I realize the danger of spiraling out of control mentally unless I can find a way to interrupt the cycle and regain a sense of equilibrium.

Chapter Twenty
Steppin' Out

Often there comes a time in life when the downward spiral of despair and depression brings one to that place known as "rock bottom." Dark and dingy, its putrid stench and filthy air keep constant company with one's pain and misery—they're your loyal companions for as long as you stick around and they want nothing more than to watch you squirm and suffer. They delight in this--it amuses them in a sick, tainted way.

Hitting rock bottom is daunting and utterly exhausting. One loses the fight in this hell hole *or* refuses to be swallowed up by this beastly bitch and realizes there's nowhere to go from here but up. It's the sheer willingness to give life another shot because you've literally got nothing more to lose...truly at a crossroad, I know in my heart that huge changes are necessary if I want not only to survive, but to thrive.

About this time and by no coincidence, I discover a book by Carol Ritberger titled *Healing Happens With Your Help.* In it the author states the following regarding left-sided breast cancer: *This is one illness where allopathic and behavioral medicine agree; both consider cancer to be the disease of nice people, meaning there's a higher predisposition for it in those who suppress their feelings and emotional needs, who are inclined to avoid conflict at all costs (even at their own expense) and who tend not to make demands on anyone because they don't want to be seen as a burden or too needy.*

While usually considered a desirable and admirable quality, self-denial tends to suppress the expression of emotions, personal needs, and desires. This type of behavior encourages martyrdom and supports the fears of abandonment and rejection. Thus, the associated emotions are loneliness, hopelessness, helplessness, pessimism, resentment, powerlessness.

Talk about summing up one's life in a nutshell! If Ritberger's words didn't hit the nail on the head, I don't know what could! These desperate adjectives depict *me, my* life, and *my* feelings-- day in and day out.

The psychological analysis of breast cancer is that it is as much an emotional illness as it is a physical illness, I continue to read Ritberger's book with amazement. *The repression of emotions has been linked so closely that it is considered to be a risk factor. Breast cancer in the left breast indicates self-directed disappointment and self-dislike. They're disappointed in themselves; their life, and their ability to find the love they need. They feel like they're not good enough and emotionally inadequate. They're tired of trying to please everyone at the expense of their own needs. There is a lack of joy and happiness in their life.*

It's as if this was prefaced with "I'm talking to *you,* sista!" It *is* me, and there's no getting around it. My cancer manifested in my left breast and I've always felt like a complete and total disappointment--to myself, my family, and the world. Essentially, I'm a failure, and a great one at that!

I understand now I'm required to step outside of the box, out of my comfort zone if I want to change things up. It occurs to me that maybe I should integrate new, complementary therapies into my treatment. So when my sister Joanne suggests acupuncture to alleviate my pain and anxiety, I think *what the heck, I've got nothing to lose...*yup, those are my exact words. In other words, I am open!

Frankly, uneducated about complementary therapies prior to my diagnosis, I simply never had any reason to explore them-- until now. Struggling with anxiety, depression, and insomnia-- extremely common ailments after one has been diagnosed with cancer—I'm embarrassed to admit that I need assistance. At this point, I have pills for sleep, anxiety, depression, pain, and nausea. The pain medication dulls my pain *and* my brain and leaves me in a fog. Sleeping pills send me into a temporary state of amnesia and I wake up feeling like a Martian--out there, somewhere in the twilight zone, but clearly not here. It's a yucky feeling and I wish there was something else I could try that might leave me feeling at least half-way human.

I know that complementary therapies are health treatments that don't fit into my home turf of standard western medicine protocol, but that some say can be extremely beneficial when used in conjunction with mainstream medicine. In short, these therapies are vastly different for someone who's never veered off that path, ventured out, or marched to the beat of a different drum, and might be quite nerve-wracking.

Still, I have to be willing to expose myself, let people in, and trust that I am supported in life. All I know is that something or someone buried deep within is kicking and screaming *I want out! There's got to be more to life than this! After all, who am I saving? Who am I protecting--really? Have I been kidding myself all along?* The even more powerful question is this: Can I drag myself out of this snake pit? Is it even possible?

Martha, the acupuncturist, is gentle, softhearted, and caring. A nurse like me, I am instantly at ease with her. Funny how we connect that way. She palpates my chi, or energy, to my liver and kidneys, and discovers both are very weak. I'm not surprised. She tells me exactly what she is going to do before inserting needles into the appropriate areas. I barely feel a thing--compared to what I've been through over the past few months, this is a piece of cake!

I'm amazed at how relaxed I feel during and after the session, and my pain level decreases immeasurably. Thankful--for chronic pain can be quite debilitating as it wears on your mental and emotional well being--the relief I feel is tremendous. It gives me something I haven't felt in a very long time, or perhaps ever: *Hope!* Acupuncture becomes part of my treatment plan and, as I opt for weekly treatment, my body responds with enthusiasm...

Martha also introduces me to relaxation breathing--one of my first holistic exercises. Easy to learn and so simple, this becomes my favorite healing technique. I take in a deep, slow breath and envision that a big red balloon in my belly inflates my abdomen and extends my belly. When I exhale the balloon deflates and my abdomen slowly returns to its natural state. I'm so much calmer after five minutes of doing this exercise! When a thought intervenes during the process, I dismiss it quietly and refocus on my breath. I can't believe how my daily routine of negative thoughts is interrupted by something this simple! I welcome the relief of silence and solitude, even if only for a few minutes...

Soon I use this technique everywhere--at home, waiting for my radiation appointments, before tests and exams--even before biopsies, of which I've had more than I care to count. It gives me a sense of well being and feeling centered, especially when it comes to my thoughts, which I once believed were bigger than me.

At Joanne's suggestion I pay a visit to a nutritionist also--one she's seen in the past and highly recommends. Thea, not only a certified nutritionist, is also a medical intuitive and a kinesiology practitioner. Sounds complex, but it isn't. Thea uses her remarkable intuitive abilities to ascertain the cause of a condition, then complements it with muscle testing--or kinesiology, a form of feedback to gain valuable data about the client and her body. I am over the top interested in all of this as I desire foods that will nourish my body. My appetite has been poor to non-existent, and I know from nutrition class back in nursing school that eating healthy plays a large role in one's healing process. In fact, it's crucial!

Thea starts me on a detoxification program to eliminate any unwanted viruses, parasites, and bacteria from my gastrointestinal tract. Done with the assistance of supplements and dietary changes, once all the toxins are removed we can move on to the next phase, known as rebalancing. Here I will be given tools, supplements, and foods that will bring my body back into balance and restore it to wellness. The information makes perfect sense and I am beginning to enjoy participating in my care. I am *definitely* on the right track now...

I begin to learn that most of these therapies view one's health from a holistic or "whole picture" point of view and can help restore the body's natural equilibrium and balance. In turn, quality of life can be improved and side-effects from cancer treatments lessened.

Another technique I learn to help calm myself is called guided imagery. Guided imagery--or healing visualization—allows you to use your own imagination to heal your body and mind. Guided imagery induces feelings of strength and peace. My personal visualization, tailored specifically for moi, suits me perfectly and proves to be extremely powerful. Incredibly, my imagination and I team up to expedite my healing journey.

I picture in my mind's eye, a bright white light entering the crown of my head and funneling down into my body, eliminating any cancer cells that no longer serve me. This magnificent light regenerates back to perfection every organ it touches. My immune system, amped up by the sparkling white light, is now on high alert. Like a pack of hungry wolves, Pat's fighter cells will no longer allow intruders! I rest in this tranquil state for ten minutes to an hour per session depending on my needs. Yes, *my* needs!

I decline hormone replacement therapy--post-radiation treatment--as recommended by my oncologist Dr. S. We don't see eye to eye on this, but Dr. S. is good with my decision. I want full compliance, nothing less--you know the drill. I want my team all on the same page!

Instead of hormone replacement therapy, I choose to ingest recommended supplements formulated specifically for me (determined by muscle testing) in addition to foods that influence estrogen metabolism. Cruciferous vegetables become a household word and the list includes kale, cauliflower, cabbage, broccoli, and Brussels sprouts. Chock full of vitamins, minerals, and anticancer properties, I grow to appreciate these healing foods, which I consider plant medicines. I begin to incorporate lignans, or flaxseeds, into my daily routine. Flax increases the fiber in my diet, which in turn eliminates toxins from my colon and aids in estrogen metabolism, as well. Other supplements help boost my immune system, which I instinctively know without a doubt has become ravaged over the years from unhealthy fad diets and poor eating habits.

I add spices such as tumeric, cumin, basil, garlic, and rosemary to my cooking. These make my food come alive and, for the first time in ages, the life force within me appears to awaken. The fact that I am involved in my care, and am not just a bystander but a participant in my recovery, is quite empowering! Still new, still fresh, and there's much to learn, but I'm willing!

Even though I limit my reading about breast cancer on the Internet, this is where I find the Healing Garden located in

Harvard, Massachusetts. This sanctuary is a rejuvenating environment for those affected by cancer and dedicates itself to providing therapeutic services and support. I think of the Healing Garden as my tranquil home away from home.

It's here that I meet Lisa, a reflexology energy healer, and am very drawn to her energy/vibration. Reflexology is the application of pressure to areas on the feet which correspond to organs and systems in the body. It is believed that applied pressure to these areas can greatly benefit a person's health. Lisa's demeanor is calm and soothing, and I recognize I am her exact opposite. Rigid and uptight, I for sure am a product of the environment in which I grew up. Being on guard 24/7 during my childhood, I've learned that chaos breeds more chaos unless you break the cycle. An observation, not a judgment on my part, it is what it is and I give myself two thumbs up for attempting to do differently in order to *feel* differently! I take another step up the ladder and out of the dungeon of darkness...

I adore Lisa because I feel so respected in her presence. She acknowledges all of me--my feelings, thoughts, and emotions, and allows me space to experience any and all of them without shame, blame, or guilt. It's safe for me to let go and feel. *Did you hear that?* I didn't think I could ever feel anything appropriately. My body and mind start to unwind, and places within which have ached for years begin to feel soothed and serene.

In this most tranquil environment, I don't feel like a number in the deli line or a guinea pig at the trough with other mammography patients. Treated like a human being, the "whole" of me is tended to, not just my left breast or the pain in my right side. This is incredibly huge, believe you me...and the cost of Lisa's sessions are factored on a sliding scale basis.

"This is what I would normally charge, but pay what you can--I am giving back and that's why I do this work," are her exact words. I kid you not! An angel, she not only assists my body to heal, she teaches me about life and that I have choices--especially when it comes to my healthcare. I begin to feel like the pieces of Pat's Humpty Dumpty puzzle are being put back together again. Like perhaps--just perhaps—there's hope for me after all...

Although not a big believer in complementary therapies before my breast cancer diagnosis, for sure I am one now! The blending of western medicine with complementary treatments is a great fit for me. I love treating the whole me--body, mind and spirit!

I learn from my experts--Thea, Martha, and Lisa--and they all recite the same exact message: "It's all about you now, Pat. You need to put yourself at the top of the list, for you are the number one priority in your life. No, it's not *selfish,* it is *selfless.*"

Hmmm....maybe—just maybe—it's time for me to take baby steps...I realize one thing's for certain: I am learning to pay attention to my body and its infinite wisdom and healing power. I think steppin' out is gonna be quite fruitful!

Chapter Twenty-One
Out of Sync

Still, some days are filled with doom and gloom—I can't minimize that fact, as there are occasionally times that prove agonizingly unbearable. I "ball my eyes out," a lot--thought I'd never stop some days, but always, in the end, I do. Funny how that works...crying is cathartic. Tears release toxins, and increase natural feel-good chemicals that help elevate my mood, so it is a huge stress reliever. God knows we all have more than enough stress in our lives! The shedding of tears actually heals the heart and soul. Crying lets the critters out, before they wreak havoc elsewhere in the body.

October 8, 2003, turns out to be the monumental day I embark upon my spiritual journey and finally begin to speak *my* truth. Unplanned—truly, I swear!--in crisis I put an "SOS" call out to the universe. This plea for help--out of sheer desperation-- starts with a simple phone call.

"Aunt Marguerite," I whisper into the phone's receiver. "It's me, Pat."

"Is everything all right?" I hear my aunt say.

Oh God, should I tell her what's happening? Maybe she's too old to handle this...and her health is failing. What the heck am I doing? This is a horrendous idea...

Suddenly my so-called "inner voice" pipes up out of nowhere once again. *Pat, Aunt Marguerite is the holiest person you know. She's as close to God as you're ever gonna get! She almost became a nun, remember? She can handle this! Just say it. Tell her your truth!*

"No aunt, I'm not okay!" That voice inside of me takes the reins and delivers one of the most pivotal statements of my life. I let the words spill out of my mouth: "I'm far from okay--I'm really sick, and I'm so very frightened! Can you pray for me please?" There--I said it! I truly don't know where it all comes from but it's as if parts of me long disconnected reunite for the first time.

"Thank you for your honesty, Pat, and for sharing your deepest fears with me," my aunt replies. "As soon as I hang up the phone I will start a prayer chain for you. I'll invite my fellow parishioners and friends to join in and raise you up to the highest power. You will be at the top of the list. We are here for *you* now. Know how special you are, dear one..."

Upon hearing my Aunt Marguerite's final words I hang up the telephone and plunge my head down onto my arms and weep and weep. So touched am I by this woman's undying love for me--this sweet lady who welcomed me into her life as if I was her own child after my mom and dad died—that I knew she was, without a doubt, a direct disciple of God! How fortunate can one be?

Prayer had been absent from my life for years, but now seems like the opportune time to open my heart to my long lost friend-- and his, or her, name is God.

God, I can no longer handle this burden alone! Please ease my pain and lighten my load. I surrender my fears to you and trust that everything will work out for the highest good. My faith is in your hands and I know you won't abandon me. I patiently await your signs. Thank you for listening. I won't take up any more of your time...

Wow, did I just surrender to a higher power and completely let go? Is it scary? Yup, won't lie about that! A leap of faith? You bet!

I doubt I've ever been connected to that part of God within me, *my spirit*...and begin to gently remind myself that God or "source," is pure unconditional love, and that "source" loves me and everyone else on the planet just the same, no matter the circumstances or from where we hail. I start to see how my own health crisis is presenting me with the opportunity to stop doing things that are not congruent with my own spiritual truth. I remain strong as I continue my quest. There's no turning back now and I reach out again...

Dad, can you hear me? It's me, Pat. Can you come to my side please? I need you asap! I'm struggling, Dad, and I don't know if I can hang on much longer!

I feel his angelic presence around me almost immediately. Although I've seen only a glimpse of what is available, my ability to connect with loved ones on the other side has been nothing but a positive, loving experience for me. The living room lights flicker and create a most sacred dance, as his energy darts from one side of the room to the other, turning shades of magenta purple to lemon yellow.

What a dazzling show! His alluring movements remind me of the hummingbird that zig-zagged from flower to flower during the final days of his life. How he'd fallen head over heels in love with this tiny creature and what serenity it had brought him before he died! Somehow, it appears Dad is trying to convey a message, and a rather compelling one at that! I continue to watch the light show, and suddenly experience an *aha!* moment which arrives telepathically. Can't really explain it...it's just a knowing.

Dad is offering me an opportunity to awaken to a new way of life on earth! His energy touches my skin and sends a rippling wave down my spine that electrifies me, and leaves me tingling all over. The hummingbird metaphorically symbolizes taking in the nectar of life, and reminds me to seek the goodness and celebrate the beauty of each new day.

Live your life with intense sweetness, Pat--take it all in! is what I know Dad is attempting to convey. And with that he is gone, and I am left, speechless.

Happy birthday Dad--I love you! Today, October eighth, will be etched in my heart forever! It was on this day your own mother gave birth to you, and now you have breathed new life into me! What a celebration this has been; what a phenomenal gift you have just given me!

And with that, the extraordinary happens--mystical and magical, literally beyond words! Something inside of me shifts, transforms, though I can't say exactly what--almost like a metamorphosis! The date, the timing, is too perfect, too coincidental--the "God bumps" pop out all over my arms and legs and I realize this entire scenario is a manifestation of the divine. Holy cow! Now in the flow where miracles and great mystery abide, I'm suddenly able to accept the gifts from all my experiences, and trust there is a higher power...always watching over me, for my highest good...

In a flash I realize that everyone carries within themselves a piece of the divine and how comfort derives from connection with this higher power! *Is it possible that when one has faith and commits to a spiritual practice, then tranquility and inner strength—strength that one never knew existed--arises? No more struggle, or searching outside oneself--for everything one needs is within and comes through source? Tapping into that wisdom can one find her inner "ding?"*

Suddenly I feel a tremendous sense of relief, like ten enormous rhinoceroses are lifted off my shoulders. For the first time since my diagnosis I acknowledge my deepest, darkest secrets. I reach out to others, instead of retreating to my mental prison. I choose not to go this alone anymore. I am flowing with the tide instead of against it! This is indeed a *revelation!*

It gets even better, for I now crave food. Let me reiterate— I'm not only actually hungry, I'm *famished!* At the same time I realize this is actually part of a huge shift occurring in this sacred moment. At my request, Todd brings home a huge BLT sandwich with greasy French fries! He must think I'm absolutely crazy! He doesn't know what to make of this sudden change, and neither do I. All I know is that I'm starving! I devour the entire meal, barely coming up for air. I can't believe it--I haven't eaten a full meal in months! And greasy, fatty foods--am I nuts? *Bad move, Pat, you'll pay for it big time,* I think...

Several hours later I lie in bed and wait for my nocturnal terrors to return. *What time this evening will the enemy known as pain come to haunt me? Will my first visit be at one a.m., or perhaps two? And every two hours after that until I awaken tomorrow, drained and weary? That's the typical pattern I've come to know and despise. No wonder I detest night time!*

Instead, I fall into a sound sleep and begin to dream. Ah... yes...I've been here countless times--helpless, alone, vulnerable, weak, hopeless, and, yes, abandoned. It's like I'm sinking in quicksand--with no way out—into a bottomless pit, swallowed completely up. It sucks the very last breath out of me until there's nothing to do but surrender. There are simply no other options. I give in to it all; my mind is no longer in the driver's seat. Something or someone else has taken over, and I'm submerged now in *darkness*.

I rock and roll through the tumbler of life, jolted around until I can't see or think straight any more. My senses fray and my hard wire disconnects. I wonder: *Am I still alive or have I died?* All becomes quiet in a heartbeat as my body lies motionless and my eyes open gently. *Dare I look around? What will I see? Where am I?*

The scene is serene. The pungent aroma of lilacs in the air, my eyes witness the brilliant cobalt blue sky floating above me. The wind whispers sweet words into my ear--words of kindness, benevolence, and affection. A blade of green grass tickles my cheek as I roll sideways into a seated position. Mother Earth beneath me, I feel like I've never felt before, supported and anchored to her very core. She envelops me in her arms, holds me close, and I feel protected and safe. My sense of abandonment vanishes, and with it, my fear...

"When did you get here, Mother Earth?" I inquire, mystified.

"I've always been right here with you," she responds, and smiles lavishly. "You've merely forgotten."

Eyes wide with wonder, I'm like a newborn colt--wobbly on my feet as I stand to salute life and all its glory--fresh from my mother's womb.

I have arrived...am I dreaming or is this really happening? I tweak myself back into reality. "It doesn't really matter," I hear myself sputter. "For in this moment, I am a new being, resilient, empowered, and filled with love and peace. I have emerged shiny and unscarred-- *alive!*" Fully awake now, I realize I'm lying in my bed in the same position in which I went to sleep. Haven't budged an inch! I open my eyes to the most glorious sunrise I've ever seen as heavenly white light streams through my window. I bolt upright in bed and scream at the top of my lungs like a little kid on Christmas morning: "*Pain free!* For the first time in months I slept through the night pain free!"

I wake up Todd accidentally with my shrieks of delight. He doesn't know what to make of me! For all I know, maybe he thinks I've gone over the edge, completely lost it! I wasn't far from that point, as you well know. Todd looks like he's just seen a ghost. Who is this chick--this woman, my wife--and what in God's name is she bellowing about at six a.m.? I can tell my face says it all, as he smiles a huge smile back at me. He looks so relieved, which is a welcome sight to behold!

I squeeze myself again to make sure the past twenty-four hours have not been *all* dream. I jump out of bed, make my way to the kitchen, and prance around the room like Ebenezer Scrooge on Christmas day. Nothing short of *a miracle* has transpired, and my life--as I've come to know it-- will never be the same! *I'm alive and well, I've been given a second chance at life!* I promise myself: *I won't screw it up this time!*

Chapter Twenty-Two
The Ultimate Gift

FORGIVENESS
by Barry S. Maltese

If you try to reach inside of your heart
You can find forgiveness, or at least the start
And from that place where you can forgive
Is where Hope and Love also thrive and live

And with each step that you try to take
And with that chance that your heart might break
Comes so much happiness, and so much strength
Which alone can carry you a fantastic length

For hate and anger will not get you there
And though you say that you just don't care
You can easily avoid the pain on which hate feeds...
The kind of hurt that NO one needs

Just make the move, take that first stride
Let go of the thing known as "foolish pride"
Maybe then you can start to repair the past
Into something strong, that will mend and last!

Pissed off at my parents for what I perceive to have been a horrendous childhood—their throwing away our childhood photo albums in a fit of wrath was merely one more proof!--I resent the fact that I lost my youth to my parents' destructive ways and had been forced to grow up too fast. Furious, I blame myself for becoming a friggin' co-dependent and allowing them to sabotage my thoughts, emotions, and actions. Why did I wait so long to break this vicious cycle of martyrdom and affliction?

I ruminate perpetually on these thoughts with much melancholy and regret for what might have been but never would be. I spent countless years obsessing over the question: *Why me, why poor, poor, bad me?*

Lethal shame, blame, and guilt are my allies, and together we comprise a pitiful group conceived out of desolation and dejection. *Rejection* our claim to fame; the truth of the matter really stings, and boy does it hurt! However, in the midst of all this chaos something inside me does an about face, transforms dramatically, and I become cognizant that I have a voice, a *say* in all this confusion. I begin to ask hard questions of myself:

Pat, why are you allowing the past to control you still? Mom and Dad are gone...they have no hold over you anymore! Move on with your life, and for God's sake, quit playing the role of the sacrificial lamb! It doesn't suit you any longer! Get busy living--or get busy

180

dying...it's up to you!

This is an unnerving--but liberating--time in my life. Indeed, it's a process that requires patience, conviction, and commitment. However, I know it's time to sever this ball and chain from around my ankle forever. Can't explain to you how I know, just take it from me, I do!

Aware I still harbor resentment and hurt--it hangs out in my body, in my cells--anywhere it can latch on and make a ruckus. Grief and sadness literally erode my sense of self worth. Still dormant negative memories and emotions will remain that way unless I shift my thoughts and attitude. Unless I make a conscious effort to forgive, I'll remain shackled forever, purgatory bound.

I've already begun to understand the incredibly powerful connection between the mind and body, known as the "mind-body connection." By harnessing the power of this connection I examine the concept of being able to use my thoughts to positively influence my body's physical responses and to promote its ability to heal.

Little by little I realize forgiveness is a gift one gives to oneself. Anger, hatred, and animosity don't hurt anyone else anywhere near as much as they hurt me. They affect me on all levels, and prohibit me from experiencing true love and pleasure in my relationships. I learn that I can forgive, not to let others off the hook, but to let myself off the hook! Forgiveness gives me permission to release any angry messages stuck in my heart and mind.

"If you are seeking revenge you better dig two graves," according to an old Chinese Proverb. I kid you not! Forgiveness doesn't excuse any of their wrongdoings—let me make that perfectly clear. It's not about making excuses or condoning one's behavior. Many times an incident long-forgotten by the abuser leaves the so called "victim" still fuming years later, carrying around hurt and sorrow. I'm learning how forgiveness might free me from emotional baggage that otherwise can weigh me down and possibly even kill me—*literally!*

How do I begin my process to forgive? I read books, and find mentors and healers who guide and support me emotionally, mentally, and spiritually. In the beginning I write nasty, vicious letters to my parents--I want them to hear every gory detail about the dreadful pain they caused. Part of me desires for *them* to feel the same mental anguish I endured day after day. I want them to hurt *real bad.* A sick kind of retaliation, I guess.

The funny part is that my parents are deceased — how can they possibly know what I'm feeling now? Dead or alive, what difference does it make? It doesn't matter to me as I continue with my exploratory process. I write letters then tear them up in a wild frenzy. Others I torch with a match and watch my words go up in a cloud of smoke. Sometimes I wail like a blubbering idiot. On other occasions I scream and yell at the top of my lungs, and curse their names repeatedly. You can well imagine what I call them isn't dainty or charming! I can't even repeat it here, so pitiful is what I say! But I'm releasing all the pent up emotions I'd pushed down into my belly years before. It's a dynamite letting go party! Truly cathartic, it leaves me feeling lighter, and free.

How long do I carry on this way? Until I have nothing left! Until I fall to my knees, exhausted, and ask for guidance, a new perspective, for God's help! I tell my story to anyone who'll listen and try to comprehend the meaning behind my life's drama--until finally I experience a second *aha!* moment.

A teacher told me once that my parents had done a perfect job teaching me the lessons *"you came here to learn."* I glared at her like she was practicing voodoo or something satanical, but she repeated herself emphatically.

"Pat, you contracted with your parents long before you incarnated onto this earth in order for you to learn this most valuable lesson called *self-love*. They performed their roles to a 'T.' They did exactly as planned and indeed, they were right on!" The light bulb goes off as I now finally understand what she meant. My parents needed to do what they did so that I could learn how to love *me*. Sounds incredibly strange, I hear you thinking, but believe it. As God as my witness, it's the truth...

Through their teachings I am learning that I am at the center of my circle of love. Self-love does not come from without, it comes from within. Self-love is the connection to my higher being, universal energy, source, and it's what makes me divine...and rare. Nothing and no one outside of me can ever--*ever*--give me that kind of love. It's simply not possible! This is an epiphany and the impetus for a fresh start. Without my parents' assistance I wouldn't have had the opportunity to get to know myself as this precious child of the Creator that I *am*. Now, that puts a different spin on my life, does it not?

Next, I begin to work on forgiving the most important person of all--m*e*. Forgiveness is about creating an opportunity for healing to begin, and for self-love to fill every crevice of my being. It's the ultimate treasure to receive, and the most splendid present I can share with others once my cup is full...remember, self-love is completely about *me!*

Eventually I come to a greater understanding of my parents, their actions, and the fact that they did the best they could with the tools they'd been given by *their* parents. They taught me what they knew--what they'd been programmed to believe to be true. Much of it stemmed from the abuse and fear they too had endured.

Time for me to let go of the "woe is me girl" and take responsibility for my part in all of this--for I played a role as well. Sometimes those who are the hardest to forgive are our greatest teachers. Now, with great humility, I thank my parents for teaching me to let go of my past and to live in the moment. Doing so brings me to a place of pure peace, a cosmic consciousness that I call *bliss...*

JOURNAL ENTRY

Dear Dad:

Thank you for teaching me to love myself, and to be patient and compassionate. Oh yeah, and one more thing, Dad--thank you for being such a pain in the ass and pushing me to reapply to nursing school because I didn't get in the first time! I wouldn't have done that without you. And I am one fine nurse today, let me tell you! Who says so? I do!

Dear Mom:

Thank you for teaching me how to take back my power and to speak my truth. It has indeed been a grand lesson, and one I have passed on to your wonderful grandchildren, Colleen, Erin, and Patrick James. You'd be so proud of them! I already know that you are, as I feel your presence around them all the time.

Since Mom and Dad passed I've learned to connect with them on the other side through a simple, easy process called *automatic writing*. Automatic writing is exactly what it says; writing without thinking about what will be said. I open myself up to receive comforting messages from spiritual beings or loved ones and put the message to paper. The information is not coming from me, just through me!

I find deep contentment in this space between both worlds. If one is open to the infinite possibilities of this universe and the pure energies it holds, I cannot express enough the comfort and solace one may find here. Wisdom, encouragement and faith are a few of the gifts one can receive by using this process!

Dad's message to me:

Dear Pat:

Where to begin, so much to say...I humbly regret the relationship we never had. I'm sorry for so much, but what I'm most remorseful for is not showing you love. I apologize that I could never give you the love and support every daughter deserves to receive from her dad. I'm sorry I didn't provide you a home where you felt safe and where you could entrust me with your heart and soul. I'm sorry I burdened you with my problems, and by doing so you were never allowed to be a kid. You were so often the parent, and your mother and I your children. I'm sorry I never told you how special you were, how extraordinary, what a gem you were... a diamond in the rough!

I have no excuses. I am guilty as charged. I know we made amends (sort of) when I died, but I completely and fully understand now that I am on the other side the seriousness of my actions--or lack thereof. I take full responsibility for everything, and am learning here in heaven how to love myself so I can open my heart to others.

I can tell you at this very moment how I do feel about you. First of all, I love you with every fiber of my being. I am so very, very proud of the beautiful woman you have become. You are a phenomenal wife, mother, sister, nurse, and healer. You touch so many peoples' lives, you give them courage and hope. You are truly a piece of God. You are a woman of tremendous strength, as I see the numerous challenges you have overcome and how it inspires you to reach out to others. Always giving, but now you take care of yourself first and foremost. Kudos to you for that!

I expect nothing from you at this time. If you can ever forgive me fully for my wrongdoings, I am here. But that is totally up to you. You have been the best daughter for whom any father could ever ask. My crossing over into the spiritual world was indeed one of your greatest contributions to me. I thank you for that as it truly eased my transition. There was absolutely nothing to fear. I bid you farewell for now. But know I am here any time you need me. I wish you nothing but abundance, perfect health, and happiness. You are worthy of it all!

All my love,
Dad

I try to remember to forgive every day. It keeps me connected to my Creator and those I love dearly on this earthly plane and in heaven. It helps me to stay grounded and to focus on my path as I meander my way back home. My relationship with my dad continues to blossom, and I've long since forgiven him as I recognize it was all for my highest good. All is well!

Chapter Twenty-Three
Finding True Love

How do I start to love myself? Very gingerly and with kid gloves! Understand it's a foreign concept, like learning a new language or riding a bike. It takes time and a lot of patience. Slow...easy...gently and lovingly.

I begin to notice how I speak to myself. In other words, I listen in on self-talk. Shocking the things I say day in and day out! What unkind words I have to *stop* repeating and change to something more positive and present tense. So I look in the mirror one day and say out loud, "I love you, Pat!"

Feels peculiar, but that's okay. Initially, saying "I love you, Pat," doesn't mean much, but I continue the ritual anyway. Remember, I'm the only one who can change it, and the process takes time. After all, how many of us say loving, respectful words to ourselves on a daily basis? Too few of us, I bet...I remain vigilant to the practice and watch in amazement at the results...

Once again journaling or drawing to release old, unwanted emotions and pent up feelings is suggested to me.

"Write from your heart," a teacher recommends.

"What does that mean?" I reply.

"It means to speak from your heart and not your head."

"But how?"

"Feel it, don't think it, as all authentic answers always come from your heart, where truth lies," she continues. "Through journaling you'll be able to express your feelings in a healthy, appropriate way without being criticized. This will assist you to recognize your emotions, validate them, and release them. Pat, when you stuff your emotions or unresolved feelings by denying or silencing them, they literally stay stuck in your body," she explains.

"If you do not release these feelings they can begin to cause discord within a particular region of the body and ultimately lead to symptoms and/or disease," she continues. "Physical pain sometimes surfaces shortly after the experience of emotional trauma because we do not express and let go of our emotions related to this trauma. It can be hugely cathartic if you are willing to peek beneath the layers of emotions that have been stored in your cells and tissue for a lifetime."

For sure, this is a lot to swallow! Did stuffing my emotions cause my cancer? No! But did it help create the perfect environment to allow this insidious disease to manifest? Most definitely! I begin to see how emotion can lie at the root of illness.

I purchase the most mouth-watering pastel pink journal I can find, one with an adorable little angel on the front cover. It calls to me immediately. Let's just say we're acquaintances at first, and rather quickly establish a solid friendship. I tell her my oppressive, gloomy secrets, and feel safe doing so. Never a judgment or criticism in her company; I trust her with my life. That's just how it is. Journaling becomes a sacred part of my day--a gentle place to fall where I somehow always feel support.

JOURNAL ENTRY

My whole life I lived as a prisoner of my own thoughts and feelings, a silent lamb unable to speak up for myself. I detested every bloody minute of it, and recognize now what pure torture living in my head has been. Sadly, I had no means of escape—until now...

I am a silent lamb no longer. Alas, I am rising out of purgatory's burning fire and rescinding my oath to the devil. May he rot in solitude and fester in his own chagrin! I'm out of here--watch out world, a tigress is being born! A pussycat no more, I'm tellin' you: Listen up and hear me roar!

On any given day if I don't feel like putting words on paper I allow my colorful markers to do the talking. I possess no true artistic ability, but my sketch pad doesn't care. It asks only that I communicate with conviction and integrity. No more false pretenses, no more lies. This I am most willing to do. I honor myself for who I am--good, bad or indifferent, for that is all of me. I begin to see I'm headed in the right direction...

Journaling and sketching encourage me to look within and heal the deep wounds paralyzing me since childhood. Time to peel back the layers to find the real *me!* I learn, after so many years of silence, that I can sob, scream, or punch a pillow, as it allows me to release pent up frustrations. I understand slowly that it's okay, and that the feelings will pass. What a relief to finally "get" that displaying emotion is *not* a sign of weakness.

Moving through my "stuff" makes me a stronger individual. I have to express the emotional drama rather than repress it, or I'll run an even greater risk of forcing my organs to shed the tears my eyes cannot. I prefer puffy eyes now over a diseased body any day.

Physical manifestation of illness is our body's way of communicating that something is awry, and emotions are our barometer. When I learn to listen to my body and understand its wisdom is infinite, I see how not getting to the bottom of what ailed me all those years is why all hell was able to break loose physically. As I release the festering, toxic thoughts and emotions from my mind, I simultaneously nourish my body, and this in turn allows me to develop new ways to cope.

Expressing emotions appropriately helps me develop greater resilience. Eventually I learn that I know my body better than any practitioner out there, and that my health situation is linked to my lack of self-love and self-esteem. As I get to the bottom of what ails me, the rewards are astounding. I settle into this new way of being and soon there's no looking back...

Dr. Bernie Siegel, a retired pediatric surgeon, writer, speaker, and an internationally recognized expert in the field of cancer says: "We must heal our childhoods and heal our wounds so our bodies can become healthy and whole again. Our bodies, in fact, know how to do just that if we let go of the pain and suffering... you must let go, for love is truthfully the emotion which will sustain you under any circumstance."

In her book *Healing Through Love*, Marilyn Innerfield writes: "Self-love is the choice to accept and honor all aspects of self as magnificent...and never to diminish, even for a moment, the perfection of who we are."

Wow, this self-love stuff really is about honoring and respecting all parts of myself and about nurturing and fully understanding that I'm worthy of achieving personal happiness and a life filled with joy! But here's the secret--the clincher--the icing on the top of the cake: Once again I begin to have mirrored back to me the fact that this love to which I keep referring, this profound love, comes solely from within and never—*never!*--from the outside, or for that matter, from anyone else...still a new theory for me to grasp at this time, I simply have to listen to my inner voice and let it sink in. It's my opportunity to release the powerful belief that I am unlovable, in exchange for freedom, joy, and peace of mind. Now I understand I am a part of the divine, and worthy of it all. Woo-hoo!

My vocabulary changes as affirmations become part of my daily routine. I learn this practice from my teacher and mentor, Louise Hay, author of *You Can Heal Your Life*. Nothing more than positive statements I repeat to myself day after day; these messages travel deep into my subconscious mind. The subconscious holds thoughts and beliefs one has about oneself and, if I allow it to, can sever old limiting beliefs and plant positive new ones. I replace my former negativity with spoken affirmations such as: "I am healthy and whole in body, mind and spirit. I am returning to wholeness. I am peaceful and calm. I am cancer-free. I am grateful for life." Always spoken using present tense, as if I'm experiencing the feeling, thought, or emotion *now*, I intend to get these thoughts to take root and grow abundantly.

Speaking loving, caring words repeatedly so that my psyche can hear them every day makes my dimples twinkle. I cherish my affirmations and appreciate their value...what cheer they bring to my once vacant and barren heart!

I write silly little love notes, and leave them around home or at work. *I am beautiful inside and out* is one of my favorites--I post it all over the house! Every time I read it, something inside of me melts, which allows the goodness to expand.

Sometimes I break into a childlike giggle. It feels so superb and so right, like the little kid inside of me is venturing out to play. That little kid takes a *huge* risk and exposes all aspects of herself, as it finally feels safe. I begin to see myself as a warrior woman whose light shines ever so brightly. My inner beauty cannot and will not stay hidden one second longer!

"I am strong, I am brave, I am courageous, I am woman, hear my thunder!" becomes my mantra. I repeat it over and over, until it slowly alters my perception of myself. Eventually, I look into the mirror and no longer view myself through ordinary eyes. Now able to see beyond the physical into my divine essence—the *true* Pat!-- this new me is all bliss and magic and grace, exquisitely delicious! There's no one else like her on the planet! Can you imagine? How sweet it is!

I realize I'll never find anyone more deserving of affection and love than me! Able to begin the journey of self exploration, I'm ready to break free from the past's stifling, rigid rules and allow my soul to shine through brightly. Only now do I begin to receive love with an open heart, and to give of myself freely and joyfully—no longer from a space of duty or obligation but from that place of pure affection and tenderness. I let go of the old so that something new and better can take its place...

I sense that previously I perceived my cup as always half empty, and attempt now to transform my perception to a cup that's half full. I envision it overflowing with nothing but goodness, and recognize that drinking from this cup—my own cup!—is more of a pleasure than a burden. I still have a long way to go with my "monkey mind," but at least this proves to be a beginning. A new beginning with endless opportunities, how mind-blowing is that!

Harnessing the power of belief in such a positive way changes my life dramatically. Once I move beyond my self-limiting beliefs, I'm able to reclaim my life. Believe me when I say the possibilities are endless: One's true self will be revealed, and the sky's the limit! It is *scrumptious,* like tasting the mouth-watering goodness of a hot fudge sundae every day!

Recognizing that free will exists in every situation encountered in life leaves me eternally grateful that I chose the path of self-acceptance and self-love.

Chapter Twenty-Four
The Sacred

One thing I know for sure: The process of dying doesn't frighten me. I have witnessed many who've crossed over with ease into the next world, including Mom and Dad. I'm not concerned about what comes after this life, for I am a firm believer in reincarnation and know in my heart I'll be reunited with loved ones again. Phew, I have to wipe the sweat off my brow after coming clean with all of that!

What's left to be worried about, you might ask? Well, I guess what has me shaking in my boots is the timing thing. I simply don't feel ready to exit this planet—*yet*! I have too much to accomplish, and so much more I want to *see!* My children--the most important people on earth to me--I want to see them get married and give birth to little babes of their own one day; I want to live out the rest of my life with my beloved husband and experience all of the pleasures I know I can if I am able to stick around for a while longer, a *long* while longer...

Most importantly, I desire to leave this earth on my own terms only and *when I say so!* How ballsy of me! But life doesn't always work out that way and this, I discover, is my biggest concern: The prospect that my life might be cut short and I could depart sooner than *I* planned.

Not fair, this game of life. You call the shots, but you *don't* call the shots. You're in control, but you're *not* in control. You're forced to deal with the hand you're dealt cuz it is what it is! How can I view this experience differently? What *is* the bigger picture? I haven't the foggiest notion, nope--not a clue...

So I sit and stew with the pain and grief about dying for some time. I feel it, taste it, whine and yell at it, become irate, sad, numb, and feel betrayed--big time! I hash it over in my heart and my head until finally I see it for what it is. It hits me and it hits me good, up one side of the head and down the other. I'm kind of dense that way sometimes, but finally it gets my attention alright!

Ironically, coming face to face with death leads me to an epiphany, a flash of recognition whereby I view things in a new light. Perhaps I'm not as afraid of dying as I am of living! I realize this sounds preposterous, but just hear me out! Perhaps it's time to fully embrace *life*!

You know the expression "get busy living or get busy dying?" I realize I'm plum sick of being the dying swan! Could it be that my biggest fear—manifested in my self-limiting beliefs--is that I don't *deserve* to live a glorious life? Maybe, just maybe, I've led myself to believe that! Looking back at my past, I realize now that we do what we know, and I wasn't raised understanding much about how to live a healthy, fulfilling life. Certainly laughter, playfulness, delight, and humor were not everyday occurrences for me! How crazy is that?

Every trial is an opportunity for growth, though I wasn't cognizant of this back then. There's always something to learn with every cobblestone I cross. If I choose, I can view any discord in my life as an invitation to release old behaviors and belief patterns that no longer serve me, in exchange for higher ones.

My God, the purpose of life is to evolve spiritually as I progress toward a higher consciousness! It's about becoming the magnificent being that God created me to be, and that I am already! I may be here to learn lessons about love, acceptance, and patience—it can be different at various times in my life. I must be willing to accept every situation and be grateful for what it has to offer me, as sometimes the most arduous adversities bring the greatest rewards...and by rewards I don't mean material stuff! I'm referring to the inner gold--security, stability, clarity, and a deep, rich, reverence for all of life. Something money can never buy!

I see now how I've agreed to each lifetime and the lessons I can potentially learn, back on the other side. I select everything, from the precise situations to the people who will play with me, so to speak. Essentially, it's all agreed upon before I arrive on the planet. The tricky part is how we forget most of the plan once we get here...as if we're stricken with adult amnesia and forget the creative beings we were on the other side! At least, that's how I see it...

In the midst of the trials and tribulations of moving forward on my chosen path, the hidden truths are revealed before my very eyes. Buried treasures that hold the key to my full potential sit within reach if I'm willing to look in those scary places and obliterate the boogey-man once and for all. All I need do is remember the truth of who I am. Unconditional love is what I was created to be and what I will always be, no matter what...

I choose to release old thoughts around the philosophy that I don't deserve a dynamite life. This assumption no longer suits me. Ironically, there's very little emotion attached to it, which signals that my beliefs no longer possess me. Symbolically speaking, the see-saw I'd teetered on for years finally begins to balance itself. I witness life differently, and the simple stuff becomes my intimate pleasures as I experience profound gratitude.

Mint chip ice cream never tasted so rich and gooey! The chirping of the robins outside my bedroom window make my ears perk up to hear the sweet symphony! The first crocuses of spring poking up through the soil elicit tears of joy--for the miracles that surround me...

Everything is truly different but nothing outside of me has really changed. *I have changed!*

All my experiences take on new meaning. I no longer sweat the small stuff. Heck, once you've been run over by a Mack truck and lived to tell the tale, these incidentals mean nothing! *Live every day as if it's your last, Pat,* becomes my new philosophy. Life is an adventure, one ginormous amusement park, and I'm not about to let it pass me by!

Saying the words "I love you" to family and friends is now a daily routine, and I love so much more deeply for it. I find greater peace with myself and the world, and my heart is open wide as I take it all in. Trust, surrender, patience, faith, and acceptance prove to be lessons that will serve me for a lifetime. I deserve all that is abundant in this universe, and that includes love, freedom, joy, and vibrant good health. It's always available simply by tapping into my higher consciousness.

Closer to God than I've ever been before, I understand now that He's always been there guiding and protecting me, but I was not awake to it. I am *awake now!* A new day has dawned-- the light has been ignited within and I am on fire!

I believe that if transformation is possible for me, then it's possible for anyone. All that's required is the willingness to take a leap of faith and *to trust.* If one has a yearning within one's soul that just won't quit--you know, that voice that won't quit sputtering to ya--that's a sign of readiness for something more. The willingness to shift perceptions and to do things differently is necessary to come to know our own greatness and to experience a reunion with the new, expanded, enlightened self!

Chapter Twenty-Five
Stepping Into My Power

I come across an advertisement in an issue of *Coping Magazine,* an informative publication that provides resources for cancer survivors and their families, and am privileged to attend a retreat called *Life Beyond Cancer* at the phenomenal Miraval Spa in Tuscon, Arizona, in 2006. A wellness retreat for women cancer survivors, *Life Beyond Cancer's* guest speakers provide an absolutely astounding wealth of knowledge. Their life-altering, stupendous messages leave me forever changed; no longer the same person in any way, shape, or form that I was upon my arrival.

It's here I meet Dr. Edith Eva Eger, a highly renowned psychologist, author, and speaker who's assisted many on their personal journey with her poignant story about her experience as a holocaust survivor. She shares her tragic yet triumphant tale to encourage individuals to let go of self-limiting beliefs and to discover their true potential. Something far out, remarkable, and phenomenal happens that afternoon at the Miraval Spa.

There is a palpable silence in the amphitheater as Dr. Edie tells her life story with compelling humility and courage:

"There are no *victims* in this world, only willing participants," Dr. Edie states. "You can't always control your circumstances, but you *can* control how you respond. Furthermore, everyone has the power to change at any time."

There isn't a dry eye in the house by the time she finishes speaking! What is it in her words that penetrate my heart and awaken me from my slumber? I don't know and, frankly, none of this matters. Remember, I'm not goin' backwards anymore. What's of greater importance, and even more far out—is that I wake up. *I get it! Cowabunga, I get it!* In that instant I make a conscious decision to eliminate the *"why me?"* from my cancer saga and propel forward in my life.

Indeed, I'd touched the center of my madness, and guess what? *I didn't die!* I'm still here! Must be a reason! Goodbye past, hello present! I'm not going to waste another minute dwelling on *what ifs* or feeling sorry for myself. Hell no! Indeed, it's most liberating to know that I'm fully in charge of my own destiny. Pat relinquishes the *victim* role *forever,* as the word no longer suits me or my story. I'll substitute the word *victor* in its place. Or maybe even *hero*—now that I'm able to see myself as a potential pioneer, luminary, and leader!

No matter what happens from this point on, I reason, I'll participate in life and in my healing process. How I arrive at this conclusion I haven't a clue, but I'm willing to commit. Commit to what? To use every resource available to me to live my best life and help me heal on every level. I'll seek out books, classes, healers, and medical experts to assist me to create a nurturing environment for both my body and mind.

To heal is to return to wholeness, and I vow that will be my intention, my mission. Passionate about this new role, and eager to empower myself and grow from this experience, I jump at the opportunity to participate in a variety of workshops that foster personal transformation and self discovery at this retreat. *This is not about surviving cancer,* I think, *but about thriving with it.* These powerful programs bring meaning to my life and allow me the adventure of being totally alive and in the moment.

Wyatt Webb, the highly acclaimed founder of the *Equine Experience,* leads a group of us on an unusual yet unparalleled excursion with his special friends--his horses--at Miraval. During his workshop I examine some of my fears as Wyatt provides a safe environment to help those of us present remember who we truly are. This provides much insight into how we communicate within our relationships, and the kind of learned behavior that often works against us.

Exasperated and frustrated one day when my horse does not respond to either my voice or the non-verbal cues I give him,

Wyatt asks: "What do you normally do with your anger, Pat?"

I feel myself get sultry and steamy under the collar-- downright irritated! *Mr. Know-It-All!* I think. *It's none of your damn business what I do with my anger! How dare you cross-examine me? I hardly even know you, and you're demanding to know something very personal--I'm not diggin this experience one bit and it's making me wicked uncomfortable...I want out of here!"*

"What do you do with your *anger,* Pat?" Wyatt repeats, undeterred. My brain goes numb, and boom, just like that, no more thoughts! But my heart is dying to speak.

"I swallow my anger--keep it inside!" I blurt at him. Soon as it's out of my mouth I can't believe I said it--I feel like I'm letting go of something bad and dirty the second I declare this out loud. No wonder I never felt whole or complete! Swallowing my emotions pretty much my whole life had literally *eaten me up.* Guilt and shame, rage and resentment are simply a few of the feelings I've held onto for an eternity. Convinced that if I speak my truth I'll be ridiculed or beaten down, now I understand this belief is an illusion--and it's time to set it free.

Wyatt pulls these illusions out of me--hallelujah! He teaches me, in the gentlest of ways, new techniques to communicate my wishes. He isn't prying at all, just doing his job—and boy, is he good at it! A kind soul who knows how to get to the nucleus--to my heart--where my goodness lies, Wyatt unleashes that piece of me once I trust and allow him in. With my newfound voice and confidence, my horse obliges respectfully and completes his part of the task at hand. Wyatt is a horse of a different color, all right! He has so much wisdom...he gets it, and he helps me to get it, too! What a personal victory today has been!

Imperative for me to speak with authenticity and no longer bury my feelings in order to remain healthy and free of disease, I reckon it will take time to alter this habit. But I have the rest of my life to do so. I didn't listen to my body until cancer pummeled me to the ground, kicked the bejesus out of me, and demanded: *Have you had enough yet?* I realize I have to shovel my horseshit today and get rid of it once and for all, as doing so just might save my life!

When I stand in my truth and integrity, it allows me to let go of all that doesn't mirror my highest intention. Releasing unhealthy situations and emotions permits my heavenly light to shine through and my whole world shifts for the better—including health, relationships, and career. I *do* have a voice, and for sure, I have options. My essence resides within--no one can create it for me. I *am* that spark waiting to be ignited, and it's lift-off time!

JOURNAL ENTRY

What a phenomenal encounter! I thought I was having a peaceful and relaxing massage. That I did, and so much more! Manny, my massage therapist rubs my entire body with lavish, aromatic scents from sweet Mother Earth. For the finale he wraps my body gently in warm, soft fluffy towels. What happens next is nothing short of mystical.

In the blink of an eye I return to the womb where I feel shelter and comfort, bathed in a cocoon of love. Not sure if this is a past life experience, I go with it. Overwhelmed by the urge to let go, I don't fight. Instead, I concede and allow. The water faucet on now, my body trembles as the releasing begins. My dear, sweet comrade Manny doesn't leave my side. He encourages me to be with my feelings and the emotions rising from within. He promises he will stay with me, and is true to his word. He strokes my hair, my head, and my back, and tells me Spirit will take care of everything. I trust this man with my life—a complete stranger, but there is something very distinct about him. I feel totally safe and free to explore. So I do. I surrender completely...

And, lo and behold, I experience a rebirth! Like a newborn baby coming into the world cherished, revered, and tended to, I emerge a radiant, powerful being of feminine energy. My body glows in luminescent colors, and love permeates my physical structure down and into the center of my being--the bosom of my soul! I feel so alive, present, and animated! A creation of God! The world awaits my arrival with anticipated adulation and affection. It's magical! Breathtaking! My grand entrance is a new beginning!

I can barely walk by the time I get off the massage table. My mind and body are mush but I don't have a care in the world! From the depth of my heart I thank Manny for this extraordinary journey we've just taken, just the two of us--and God, of course--together. As we hug for the last time, I know without a shadow of a doubt that he's been sent to me for this specific purpose on this memorable day. An angel sent from up above to fill my soul with eternal love. I will never forget you, Manny! Thanks universe!

When I let go and allow the divine and the angels to assist me, everything I release is replaced by something better, or sent back healed. I believe a part of my spirit died the day I learned I had cancer. Why? So I could abandon the old beliefs that were killing me. More importantly, so I could get busy living! Earth dwellers don't always get a second chance at life, and I'm not about to pass up the opportunity! I emerge with a new zest for the world and for me!

Everything--and I mean everything--surfaces with new meaning. A simple snowflake falling from the sky represents perfection, as does the ruby-red cardinal's sweet melodic song on a warm spring day. I will take nothing for granted again, especially my family and friends! The universe acknowledges my heart's yearning for love and to simply be love. And that, is who I am, I just know it!

Rebirth: A spiritual enlightenment causing a person to lead a new life. And holy crap, what cool events begin to unfold in my world--opportunities I never imagined possible that are too enticing to pass up.

Chapter Twenty-Six
The Firewalk

"Let us build this fire with respect for the wood, the earth, and the flame which will burn at twelve hundred degrees in a few short hours," Karen says.

Yikes, that's hot--I don't know about this! I think. *I might be giddy-uppin' outta here sooner rather than later!*

At Eye of the Hawk Holistic Center in Rye, New Hampshire, it's a crisp, cool summer's eve, and I'm not sure why I'm here, really...I saw it posted on the center's website--*Firewalk*--and I guess you could say it spoke to me. The *fire*, I mean--it drew me in, like the flickering flame of a candle! The thought of it mesmerized me, brought me to stillness. Next thing I know, I'm signed up!

How peculiar, you may be thinking. Yup, you're right on--I, too, wonder sometimes how I'm attracted to these adventurous seminars that on one hand frighten me to death, yet on the other, peak my interest to the point where I'll literally throw myself onto the fire to give it a go. I swear, I never used to be like this!

Never in my wildest dreams did I imagine walking on a bed of hot coals. But once again this mystery school called "life" presents me with an adventure I can't refuse. That's what makes this journey so doggone cool! Around every corner is a new possibility if one just says *yes!*

My girlfriend Cheryl and I arrived together, punctual as always. My dearest childhood friend agreed to play with me tonight. Yes siree, another crazy woman like me! I'm honored she's here, as she's one of my greatest supporters; like family, she's another *sista,* as I like to call her.

Our first task at hand is to create the fire. We gather wood from the barn and place it along the twelve foot-long by four foot-wide bed. Our teacher, Karen, instructs us how to proceed, as this is a crucial step in the process.

We head inside for the warm-up exercises, no pun intended. I'm feeling hot and bothered already. The adrenaline's beginning to flow. It courses through my chest--thump, thump, thumping-- and I feel my face growing beet red and ready to burst, like an over ripe tomato. I smile, though, like I'm cool as a cucumber...fat chance anyone's buying it...

Karen explains the symbolism of a firewalk, and portrays it as a tool for self discovery and personal growth. The fire metaphorically represents one's fears, negative thoughts, and beliefs accumulated in this lifetime. Walking over hot coals symbolizes the release of these debilitating fears because it reveals how - if one's personal belief system is not working in her best interest - it can be shattered into smithereens. It's a letting go...

At this point I'm learning that what I believe has a direct impact on my experiences, both mentally and physically, as well as on the outcomes in my life. My belief system can support a life filled with joy and harmony, or suffering and pain, whichever one I choose to direct my energy towards. Could it really be as simple as mind over matter? Perhaps, if I focus on the positive and the best possible results, that's what I'll get. Maybe, that's the hidden key that unlocks my door to happiness.

I hang on Karen's every word. I'm nudgy, plum antsy--my pot's getting stirred and I feel a force swirling inside waiting to be free...like on the show *I Dream of Genie*, the bottle holding my genie is waiting to be uncorked!

Karen affirms we won't do the firewalk for several hours, as the group must first prepare mentally and emotionally for this big event. Our next two exercises do just that--create mental stamina, release fears and blocks, and build a foundation of cohesiveness and trust among our team.

When Karen reveals our first exercise, our jaws drop with trepidation at what we see. *What the fuck - pardon my French,* I think. An uneasiness settles in my bones. Underneath the white sheet lies a mammoth concrete block supported by two rows of blocks on either side. *Is she out of her dang mind? I'm no rocket scientist, but I've a sober idea what this entails! Show me to the nearest exit, please!*

It's exactly as I anticipate. I'm supposed to split this ghastly block in half with my *bare hand!* I don't remember seeing "block breaking" anywhere on the website under *Firewalk Seminar!* I gaze around the room quickly at the rest of the class to ascertain what they're thinking. Some are looking cool and laid back, others giggle nervously, while a few look as if they've just seen Casper the ghost. I figure they'd like to hightail it out of here with me.

Not a soul moves, though, as Karen continues her directives. I sit up straight, perk up my ears, and pay extra close attention. She guides our group through a short visualization where I picture in my mind's eye all of my fears being poured into that cement block, then witness myself karate chopping it in half.

"Feel your hand connect to the block," Karen orders. "Hear the block fall to the floor... *see* what it will look like...picture what you will feel like...engage all your senses and watch the end result--the stupendous outcome!"

Okay, that wasn't so bad, I muse as I return to the reality of the room. The humungous friggin' cold cement block stares me square in the eye, trying to intimidate me. It's doing a great job, too--and I'm supposed to break it in half? Perhaps I should concede now, not humiliate myself, take a rain check, say *maybe next time...*

Though tight-lipped, I don't shy away. Karen asks who wants to go first, but there are no takers--not one of the ten strapping martial arts students who look like they could do this with their eyes closed. Nope, not one of them. She asks a second time and, suddenly, without warning my arm shoots up in the air. Twenty-five or so blank faces peer at me.

Guinea pig! I hear them smirking inside. *Did I just do that? I didn't raise my hand on purpose, I swear! What was I thinking? I can see it now in the local newspaper: Wacky girl shatters hand attempting to slice cement block in two! Get her to the nuthouse, not a hospital!* It happened and there's no exit now. *I have to stay, cuz something or someone won't let me leave, not yet...just do it, Pat, get it over with! Either you'll succeed or you won't, but at least you'll have given it the old college try. And that's everything!*

In a flash of clarity, I understand I'll reconcile with myself, whatever the outcome. *If it breaks, fabulous, if it doesn't, oh well.. you did your best. You've shown up and that alone takes guts!* Right there is huge growth. Lord knows I don't feel that way always. Anyway, you know this about me--it's old news!

You're most likely wondering if I have butterflies in my

FIREWALK

stomach. You bet I do! But I take those butterflies, spiders, snakes, and goblins, and tell them "get lost, scram, hit the road!" I approach the cement block and say *hello* to it silently, as if it's my long lost friend. I hope secretly that perhaps it will work *with* me, not against me, if I befriend it. Any port in a storm right now...

I take three deep cleansing breaths and exhale three huge "ha's!" as Karen has instructed. I position my legs shoulder distance apart for proper balance and alignment, and with an erect spine I stand tall and proud. Hand in karate chop position, fingers clenched and tight, like I'm in charge, I raise my hand two feet above the block, hold it steady, and breathe fortitude and stability into every molecule of my being.

Closing my eyes, I ask for guidance. *Mom, Dad, angels, universe...be here now...guide me with this and please protect me, too...especially my hand! Thank you.* I take one more deep breath, visualize that block already split in two, and repeat to myself: *I've got this...I've got this...I've got this...*

Next, I simply detach from the outcome, and with one more huge "ha!" simultaneously observe my hand strike the concrete slab and tear it in two. I continue to watch as it plunges to the floor with a whopping thud.

It happens so lickety-split fast that at first it doesn't register. I'm in a daze until I hear the thunderous applause from my classmates as they screech "You did it, Pat!" I whirl around to see my teacher smiling brightly, as if to say: *What, you're surprised? I knew you could do it all along!* I give her the biggest bear hug ever, even though I've just met her. I pump my right fist into the air six times and take a gander back at that slab of fear, broken and splattered now all over the floor. *That's some major shitola, gone forever!* I think.

Boy do I feel proud, courageous, brave, and strong! Heck yeah! This proves to be one of the most invigorating moments of my life and brings me to tears. Good tears, though. The adrenaline is surging now--bring it on, baby!

The rest of the group succeeds too. We have known each other for less than an hour but are already developing a bond, a camaraderie that boosts each other's confidence. We are a team and the momentum is skyrocketing!

Karen reveals the next morale-building exercise. This one blows my socks off! She holds up a rebar, which is short for reinforcing bar--a steel bar commonly used as a tensioning device to strengthen and hold compressed concrete in reinforced concrete masonry structures. The goal of the exercise is to pair up with a partner and bend this so-called rebar *with our throats!*

Insane, kooky, wacky, screwy--yes, to all of the above...

This activity gets everyone revved up a bit and a whole lot

more fidgety, especially the martial arts guys. They aren't lookin' so cool, calm, and collected anymore. I'm not going first this time, that's a given! My confidence level dips down a few notches, I decide to sit and watch, to see if this is even remotely worth trying.

Karen detects the anxiety amongst the group. She attempts to quell our collective restlessness by stating that this is merely another activity to help us drop self-limiting beliefs. "It's really not about the rebar," she explains. We look at the tense metal piece of iron, and I think: *I beg to differ...*

What is she smoking? Cuz here's my visual on this one: I see the bar puncturing a gaping hole in my voice box, causing me to bleed to death! No, I envision it protruding through my neck, severing my carotid artery, killing me instantly! Neither vision is appealing, it seems pretty risky, and I'm experiencing major doubts, man!

Two handsome martial arts dudes opt to go first. *Sorry saps,* my brain snorts, *or maybe they're masochists!* I hope they can't hear me thinking that gushing red blood seeping out of their throats would sure ruin their all-white attire. Tainted thoughts, I know, I know, my bizarre ideation. Just more of that "stinkin thinkin"--that's what I'm here to get rid of, remember?

They face each other and place one foot in front of the other for stability. Taking the rebar in their respective hands, they place it gently on the soft area of their necks below their voice boxes. Both men lean forward so their weight is up front, to support themselves and the bar. The goal is to move toward one another and bend the bar into a V-shape. The force of their weight, combined with faith, fearlessness, and positive vibes, should brace them and lead to their success.

"I don't think I can bear to watch this," I murmur to myself as I slap my hands over my eyes. "This is too freaky--it scares the dickens out of me!"

So I don't watch. And I wonder...and wonder...*what the hell is happening?* I don't hear gasps, shrieks, or any of the gruesome noises I'd anticipated. Instead, words of optimism and encouragement ring through the air, and when I unpeel my hands from my face I witness the most astounding sight: Two grown men jumping up and down in ecstasy, a bent bar in their hands-- they did it! They accomplished this tremendous feat, easily and effortlessly, and shattered every rule and negative belief of mine in a gargantuan way!

Still not convinced that I want to experiment with this pretty little bar, I wait and wait and wait. Waiting only builds tension, increases my apprehension. This sucks, big time.

Cheryl and I are the final two participants--everyone else has passed with flying colors.

"Are you ready? Karen asks. I don't recollect responding, only remember staring at Cheryl, six feet away, with a rebar between our necks. Obviously, somewhere between "are you ready?" and "go!" my mind/body collaborated to say *yes, we're ready!*

I shut my eyes tightly and envision the bar bending. On the count of three, we propel our weight forward to compress the rebar. Strong-willed in our desire, we mean business, but we don't achieve our objective. Cheryl lets up on the bar, and I'm thrown back. We almost had it, we really did. So close, but no cigar!

Karen tells us to take some deep breaths, and to refocus and recommit if we want to try it again. Honestly, I already feel like a winner...I really do. Cheryl and I glance at each other for a brief second, then give Karen the thumbs up sign. Hard as nails, we two avant-garde women are not conceding! We'll give it another shot...

A thought pulsates through my brain quickly: *Pat, you've faced your biggest fear, cancer...this can't hold a candle to what you've been through. So knock this one out of the park--hit a home run!*

The group begins to call our names and I feel the energy mount as a surge of toughness rises up from within. No more hesitation now, for I know what Cheryl is made of, and it's the same stuff as me--she's a tough cookie, too, so no more doubt, let's rumble!

This time we move together in synchronistic fashion. Our eyes totally focused on each other, we're relentless in our desire to accomplish our goal. Like the story of the *Little Engine That Could,* I recite in my head: *I think we can, I think we can, I know we can...* and I am dead serious. I know Cheryl's thinking the same thing, and that our positive thoughts will generate such a great vibration and force that the rebar will have no choice but to bend. Guess what? The piece of metal begins to cooperate, and this sucker starts to arch right in the center.

I hear the jubilant voices of our team supporting us in the background, and see the determination in the whites of Cheryl's eyes. We move toward each another, the bar curves even more, and I realize we got this! Hell, we're gonna do it! I feel the robustness pouring out of us both; we're swelling with well-deserved pride.

We let go of the bar, hold it up in the air, and do our victory dance. Like school girls we bob up and down, hug one another, look up at the bar and hug again. It's the most astounding feeling in the world because--as you know--I *really* had doubts about this one!

I feel my throat to make sure it's okay. By George, it's fine and dandy! I can't wait to bring that rebar home for my family to see-- they're gonna have to see it to believe it! Heck, I do, too!

The stage is now set for the finale, the *Firewalk,* and I'm pretty much on top of the world at this point. Karen gives us directions about how we'll proceed, including one very important last tidbit of information. She looks quite businesslike and her expression is dead serious.

"I hope by now that you've all begun to listen to your intuition, your gut," she says. "If it's telling you not to walk on fire tonight, then please abstain, for this is where someone can get injured. You must be *one hundred percent* certain that you are ready! If it's not this evening, there will always be a next time."

Wow, take the wind right out of our sails, why don't you? I think.

The group becomes introspective as each of us delves deeply inward for our individual answer. I, for one, will do whatever my gut tells me. I have zero pride invested in not firewalking and bowing out if need be. Heck, I've already accomplished more tonight than I ever imagined possible!

We step outside into the night, and instantly I'm drawn to the fire. Its red hot coals flicker in the moonlight, and I hear the sizzling and popping sounds of the wood. My senses become heightened. Spectacular, eye catching, sensationally wicked is this sight! Suddenly I'm revved up--really pumped! I kid you not--I'm nervous, scared, excited, and eager, but more than anything I'm aroused like you can't imagine...

222

I hang in the background for a bit and watch while some of my comrades lead the way. Many of them are experienced firewalkers--it's not their first time waltzing across a bed of blazing embers. I witness their jubilant expressions as they walk-- some laugh, some smile, and others cry, the emotions here are as unique as the people. It's quite the ceremony!

I hear the beat of drums and rattles in the distance and lose myself in the rhythm. I begin to sway with the sounds of the instruments and sweet Mother Earth as they sing their rhapsodies in unison. I find myself advancing, moving closer to my red hot friend. As I approach, I roll up my pants, remove my shoes and feel the wet, soft, cool grass beneath my feet. I peer at the glowing coals before me, greet them, and tell them how much respect I have for them, for they are truly created from Mother Earth, who is pure, unconditional love, and I trust her with my life. Not a shred of a doubt, I am ready to *walk!*

My hands folded in prayer position, I place them gently between my breasts. I recite a quick prayer of thanks for this glorious opportunity. With spine erect, chest out, chin up, eyes gazing straight ahead, I picture myself gliding over the hot coals with ease and grace. I take a deep breath, release a monumental sigh, raise my right foot and place it gingerly on the glistening coals. Carefully and methodically, I do the same with my left foot.

Slow and steady is my mantra and I'm in no hurry. I repeat the motion several times and soon my movement takes on a life of its own.

Aware once again of the drum's *thump thump!* and Karen's voice as it hums a sweet tune, my mind disconnects from my body and I'm taken on a journey to another space and time. At a ceremony that appears to be a rite of passage or initiation, I am adorned in a brilliant headpiece of colorful red, orange, and yellow wildflowers with soft white feathers and shiny leaves strewn throughout. Hanging around my neck is a felt pouch filled with small, clear crystal stones. Digging my fingers into the wet clay from the earth, I decorate my bare chest, face, and arms with the mud. Dancing wildly around the blazing fire, I kick, scream, and contort my body into some kind of frenzied but symbolic dance. One by one, I pull a stone out of my pouch, blow back and forth over it, and then toss it into the fire, symbolizing my release of old ways and beliefs.

Like a snake sloughing off its skin, I shed my fears and limitations. The drum beats come to a halt, and I rise to attention, raise my arms to Father Sky, and give thanks for this cleansing, ceremonial healing. Transformed into a rising warrior, I am strong, courageous, and full of passionate conviction...

In a split second, I become aware I'm back in my body which, oddly enough, feels vastly different. Gazing down at my feet, I think, *yup, they're hot, for sure, but there's no burning sensation, no pressure.* My legs become charged with a vibrating energy that surges up from my toes into my ankles and calves. *It's electrifying.*

I pick up the pace, raise my feet with confidence, and place them firmly on the coals. There 's nothing that can stop me now! I near the end of the firewalk and see Karen waiting for me. Her face says it all, as she's grinning ear to ear like the Cheshire cat! I jump into her arms and she cradles me like my mother did on my first day of kindergarten. Secure, protected, and loved, I am in heaven...

Tonight I firewalked through my limiting beliefs and fears--symbolized by the fire--and came out unharmed and transformed. I found a connectedness deep within my being that showed me I can accomplish anything to which I set my mind. This seminar clearly illustrated *my* potential, and the potential of every human being on this planet, and how, collectively, we can heal the mind, body, and spirit! Just imagine what an impact we could have on the entire world--*together!* What a triumphant evening!

Every day now I set my intention for vibrant health and well-being. I focus my attention on the positives in life! It's my lens and I can alter it if I don't like what I see! Change my perception and eveything shifts! That's how I create my new, rich, awe-inspiring world! *Who's* in charge? You know the answer to that one! Finally, I know I must beat the drum for my *own* heart, as it will always lead me back to Source.

Home again, I literally fall into bed, black feet and all. I don't care one bit. The feel-good chemicals still racing through my brain, I have difficultly falling asleep. It doesn't bother me that I can't snooze though, cuz I'm on a natural high and, truthfully, I don't want it to end.

The next morning, upon awakening, I question if the previous evening was an illusion. It seemed so surreal! I kick off the bed covers, raise my legs straight up in the air, and take a gander at my jet black feet. Guess not! I smirk with delight and can't wait to show my family. You're probably wondering if I did, in fact, tote that rebar home? You betcha, baby, and you should have heard the gasps when everyone saw it! I was one proud mama!!

I'm indebted to this experience--and to my incredible family, friends, the lessons, the blessings, the chaos, the drama, the cobblestones, and *yes!* even my cancer--because I know it's allowed me to dig so deeply into my fears and uncover that hidden gem: *Love!*

I reflect on my journey and again think of myself as a reformed Ebenezer Scrooge, for I've awakened from a dream. I've come full circle, and every day is like Christmas morning now--

filled with joy, pleasure, love, and miracles. I guess you could say I have an extraordinary life in the most ordinary of ways! And you know what? So richly blessed am I now, that I wouldn't want it any other way...

Chapter Twenty-Seven
Gratitude

"Everything has its wonders, even darkness and silence,
and I learn whatever state I may be in, therein to be content."
~ Helen Keller

I can't think of anyone who understands the essence of the word "darkness" better than Helen Keller. Like her, I've been in that dark solemn place, and it did not remotely satisfy me. I despised living in that kind of "hell." Alone and afraid, twisting through the haze of despair; only when I allowed myself to befriend the silence and just be still, did a shift in consciousness begin.

This shift ultimately propelled me into the light, and my perception of the whole world changed. Grace and goodness flow to me now, and continue to do so daily. There is nothing I need do to earn it, for it is indeed my birthright! If and when I find myself back in that funky, fearful place, I open my spiritual eyes and ears and intuit without a doubt that all is well. When I trust and have faith in God and the bigger picture, I recognize that a solution is always at hand. Whatever it may be, it will be for my highest good!

It's been eleven years since my diagnosis. Time has passed,

wounds have healed, and there's much for which to be grateful. Gratitude is a most powerful attitude to adopt; there are indeed hidden blessings in everything!

Now I look at a baby picture of myself, nestled graciously in the arms of my grandmother. As I gaze into my own eyes--the eyes of a perfect newborn baby--a burning question presents itself: *Must ask...the time is now,* rings in my ears. I don't second-guess my inner voice--I put pen to paper and request that my deceased mom come forth and speak with me. Instantly she's by my side, attentive and ready to provide me with what my heart has longed to hear for all of eternity.

Dear Mom:

I seek assistance on my path. Can you share with me please the story of my birth? How I, Patricia White Bateson, came to be?

She proclaims the following to me in her angelic voice:

You are a sweet child created from love. Yes, there was much fear in my life, yet divine love was present also. In my heart, I knew at the time of conception how blessed I was to have conceived you. You entered this world with a gentle cry, but possessed an inner strength and beauty that penetrated my heart. When I looked deep into your eyes I saw nothing but unconditional love, compassion, and innocence. I treasured the times I'd caress your tender body and rock you gently in my arms. I held you to my bosom and felt nothing but your magnificent love--not only for myself but for all mankind. All angst stripped away, I sensed you'd accomplish great things--that you'd help heal the world...

I share this sacred moment with you now, and want you to know that you are--and always will be--the light of my life! Fill your heart with love and let it radiate into the galaxy. Feel the love that surrounds you from the heavenly skies and the earth below. People see the glow in you, and this is what touches their very core and encourages them to engage in their own healing work. Providing that sacred space for others is how miracles occur. You've witnessed them already, have you not?

Remember, freedom is a gift; the key to unlocking your unlimited potential. You've almost taken your mask off fully. When you do, your energies will expand beyond all space and time, your divine spark will present itself fully and completely--and your inner compass will become your guidance system.

I look forward to seeing your book--this book--reach the shelves of bookstores everywhere! The healing of not only yourself, but others who seek a similar path, will prove monumental, and you will guide others back home to source...

Proclaim no longer that you weren't wanted! Destined to come into this world to recognize fully unconditional and self-love, this is a most profound lesson you chose to learn. There has never been any child more treasured than you, dear one. Your incarnation in this lifetime was purely divine timing and I was most privileged to be the vehicle that facilitated your entry. Go forth now and share your light with the world!

Eternal love,
Mom

I read this compelling passage over and over again, and my

body speaks to me with clarity through its vibration. There's absolutely *without a doubt* no longer any need to question my existence. My soul--so free and uninhibited--finally stands *alone* with the naked truth as I remember what I've forgotten eons ago. There are no more illusions, as the veil has been lifted. I see clearly now and perceive that I, Patricia White Bateson, was destined to be born on January 24, 1958, to Rita and John White - who not only anticipated my arrival, but welcomed me in their own way, with open arms! *Yippee!*

Indeed a revelation, this is *key*. My journey has brought me back to the divine spark within. Laid down gently at the feet of the Creator, I smile in sheer delight as she whispers the sweetest message I've ever heard--one of unconditional love. There's a familiar ring as it echoes throughout the chambers of my spiritual heart. I nod in agreement for now I recognize every syllable, every sound. I taste it, feel it, see it, and *know* it.

The message is: I entered this incredible world to be loved. By whom, you ask? By *me,* and *me* alone. Furthermore, the love I feel from the universe merely mirrors my own "essence" as it smiles back at me. How *cool* is that?

I continue to learn, grow, and evolve as this chapter ends and a new one begins. What lies ahead I do not know; I know only the exhilaration of this moment, for in it I am truly *alive*.

Final Thoughts

"When you were born you cried and the world rejoiced.
Live your life so that when you die, the world cries and you
rejoice."
~ Cherokee Expression

A crazy ride, this life of mine, but I wouldn't trade it for the world! I've come so far--never can I return to where I began...I've grown tremendously, love myself for exactly who and what I am, and recognize now my inner beauty. Diving head first into the darkness ultimately led me to the light. Freedom awaited me, hiding behind that facade known as pain and suffering.

One thing I know for sure: When I die, I'll die happy that at least I've given it my all and made a difference to those whom I've served. Most of all, I've loved and been loved deeply. So privileged am I, for love is the ultimate gift that can heal our planet...

When ill, my body resonated with an extremely low vibration. My energy barely sustained life. All these techniques I've shared helped raise the frequency of my energetic system and assisted my healing process. And the key? *Self-love!*

For love is the highest vibration on this planet! When I learned to love myself fully and align myself with my truth, I began to recognize my own great potential. Now I select the tools that resonate deeply with my soul and implement them. When I take care of myself physically, emotionally, mentally, and spiritually, and trust my innate wisdom and power, I gift myself the grand opportunity to return to wholeness...to balance... and vitality!

If you are like me--faced with finding your "inner healer"-- may you discover, too, that no one knows what's best for you better than *you*...when one is willing to dig deeply into the real story behind their disease, to release unhealthy thoughts and emotions, to do old things in new ways, one opens to the possibility of a shift in perspective and consciousness.

If you are sick and tired of suffering - welcome aboard - harmony, joy, and vibrant health await you as you transform your life before your very own eyes! Look beyond the distress and face freedom head on--freedom to be all that you are, just as you are. *You are magnificent!* Remember always your greatness; it's right there waiting to come forth. You have the *power,* you are the *gift!* Shine your light for all the world to see!

I leave you now with this poem I read to my students at the end of my "Healing Journey" class; *you,* as well as they, were in my heart upon its composition. *Hope* may be a small, simple word, but its rich, deep meaning allows us to feel its unlimited power— profound, and always available to you...

HOPE

Hope is what strengthens your spirit
And gives you the ability to face each new day
It is what lifts you up and gives you courage in times of
adversity
Hope is yours to keep in your safe place
It can never be taken away from you
It is yours for all eternity
Know that you have the power within yourself to heal
Never lose sight of this
Never lose HOPE

May Spirit bless you on your journey.

Namaste,
Patricia Bateson

ABOUT THE AUTHOR

PATRICIA BATESON RN, OCN, is a health care provider, healer, teacher, and author. She is a registered nurse with more than thirty-four years of experience and the past seventeen have been in oncology.

She is a cancer survivor and author of several articles published in Breast Cancer Wellness and Coping Magazine.

Patricia is a Reiki Master, Tong Ren Practitioner, Seven Levels Coaching Clairvoyant Graduate, and is certified in Basic Aromatherapy. She offers individualized private healing sessions and teaches and facilitates empowering mind/body/spirit classes. She has been a frequent guest speaker on Methuen Community Television, always seeking avenues to raise awareness, awaken, uplift and inspire others on their path.

A student of "A Course In Miracles", Pat attends Unity On The River Church in Amesbury, MA, her home away from home!

In her spare time, Patricia enjoys gardening, yoga, meditating and spending time with her loved ones. She has 3 amazing grown children, 2 wonderful son-in-laws, an incredible husband and her newest love… a delightful granddaughter… whom she considers to be her greatest teacher. Patricia resides in Andover, MA.

For more information about workshops, private sessions or any inquiries, please visit her website at **www.path2healing.us**.

NOTES

Chapter 13: Letting Go

113   *Please forgive me, I forgive you, thank you, and I love you*: Dr. Ira Byock, "The Four Things That Matter Most".

Chapter 20: Steppin' Out

157   *This is one illness where allopathic and behavioral medicine agree*: Carol Ritberger, "Healing Happens With Your Help".

Chapter 22: The Ultimate Gift

179   Barry S. Maltese, "Forgiveness".

Chapter 23: Finding True Love

193   *We must heal our childhoods and heal our wounds*: Dr. Bernie Siegel.

193   *Self-love is the choice to accept and honor all aspects of self as magnificent*: Marilyn Innerfield, "Healing Through Love".

194   Louise Hay, "You Can Heal Your Life".

Made in the USA
Middletown, DE
07 May 2015